Potomac Review

Potomac Review is a journal of fiction, poetry, and nonfiction
published by the Paul Peck Humanities Institute at
Montgomery College, Rockville
51 Mannakee Street, Rockville, MD 20850

Potomac Review has been made possible through
the generosity of Montgomery College.

A special thanks to Dean Rodney Redmond.

For submission guidelines and more information:
www.potomacreview.org

Potomac Review, Inc. is a not-for-profit 501 c(3) corp.
Member, Council of Literary Magazines & Presses
Indexed by the American Humanities Index
ISBN: 978-0-9990403-5-5
ISSN: 1073-1989

SUBSCRIBE TO POTOMAC REVIEW
One year at $24 (2 issues)
Two years at $36 (4 issues)
Sample copy order, $12 (single issue)

TABLE OF CONTENTS

FICTION

A. Kathryn Davis
THE EARLY COW 1

K.L. Browne
RED BLUFF 19

Megan E. Calhoun
THE WORKSHOP 57

Janice Deal
ANTIMATTER 97

Tyler Sones
GLORY UNDER QUARANTINE 137

Lori D'Angelo
WHAT SHE FOUND THERE 165

Tim Keppel
OZYMANDIAS 181

POETRY

Anne Hunley Trisler
FALL 12

Michael Phillips
BECOMING WATER 14

Peter Grandbois
POKING THROUGH THE VOID 16
THE INCONSOLABLE WIND 17

Louise White
WALK WITH MY FRIEND 40
HORIZON 42

Roy Bentley
EVE COMES CLEAN ON THE SUBJECT
    OF TEMPTING ADAM 43

Michele Sharpe
    OLD HOMESTEAD 52

Hari Bhajan Khalsa
    LOVE LETTER TO MY INSECURITY 54

Catherine Esther Cowie
    A NAME I WILL NOT CALL MY DAUGHTER 70
    WHEN I FOLLOW GOD'S VOICE INTO THE DESERT 71

Al Nyhart
    RUSSIA THING 72

Maryann Corbett
    NEW MEDIA 73

Katherine FAllon
    ELEVATION 91

Rita Quillen
    TEXACO OPERA 92

Tufik Shayeb
    HOW TO REINCARNATE 94

Barbara Schwartz
    PANTHEISM 113
    LOVE POEM AFTER 10 YEARS 114

Raymond Luczak
    ABDUCTIONS 116

Rachael Gay
    PANTOUM AS PROOF OF THE GENTLE 132
    3 A.M. ONE-SIDED CONVERSATION WITH MARY 134

Alejandro Pérez
    SONNET FOR SISYPHUS 160
    ARS POETICA SONNET #3 161

Connie Jordan Green
    THE QUESTION OF WHERE 162
    EVEN TODAY 163

Lisa Low
    LOVE POEM TO OSWALD 176
    ON THROWING AWAY MY DAUGHTER'S
        CHRISTMAS CARD PHOTO 177
Sarah Wyman
    LONGFELLOW HOUSE /
        WASHINGTON'S HEADQUARTERS 178
    JULY 7 179

NONFICTION

Mia Herman
    WINGS 45
Orman Day
    WHEN WE WERE SWASHBUCKLERS 75
John Talbird
    WHAT HAPPENS NEXT 119

CONTRIBUTORS 192

He sinks up to his elbows in the water and is reminded of the way he feared quicksand so constantly as a child.

A. KATHRYN DAVIS

THE EARLY COW

The cows have begun to drown themselves in the lake.

That's what the old man says, anyway. He has only a handful of teeth; popcorn kernels of black and grease. The boy nods his head, but he's never heard of any animal killing itself, not besides those tiny rodents who fling themselves from cliffs. And even they don't mean it. Or maybe they do. The boy is not sure, or can't remember.

The old man has taken to shouting, as he often has, waving his arms above his head as he stands there at the end of the drive, shouting everything but the boy's name because he cannot remember it. He has never remembered the boy's name, though it's the same as the boy's father's, and the old man has never forgotten to call the father "Caleb." The man stands now at the end of his drive with the boy, this Caleb, who'd come when he'd shouted, maybe alarmed or maybe annoyed at the old man who flailed his arms. All the same, the two stand in the melting autumn, talking about the man's cows. The skin of the man's face pulls tight against every bone like misshapen plastic. The cows have begun to drown themselves in the lake.

"Wen' missing," the old man slurs, "Went missing, 'til I saw her down there. Knew she wa'n missing no more. Just dead." The man cackles, unsmiling. He looks at the boy as if waiting for a response, but the boy hasn't got one. He wonders how much longer he'll have to stay. He is too afraid of the old man to leave. The fog hangs behind the old man who drones on in front of his blue house trailer. The fog isn't thick enough to hide the mold that crawls along its siding. It's been that way, covered in grime, since

1

Caleb's been old enough to notice, since he's been old enough to know he ought to avoid the man across the road. The fog's thick enough to mask the cows that graze and buck behind the trailer, but not so thick that Caleb can't see their outlines. Not so thick that he doesn't wonder how much a difference one less cow would make, really.

"'Elp me grab 'er," the old man says. He's asking for help and the boy will have to give it. Caleb's father says the man is batshit. His father says they've got to respect him. The old man without teeth is a veteran. He's a meth head, too, Caleb reminds his father. The father says that Caleb can't be sure of that, not really, and he says the old man is batshit, but they have to respect him. They have to help. Caleb tells his father he is too afraid of the man to help. Everyone knows he keeps shotguns; even the sheriff. The old man is a meth head, but he's not the worst of them.

"'Undred bucks?" says the old man when Caleb doesn't respond.

"What?"

"Hel' me grab 'er. Give you 'ndred bucks." Caleb is silent for a moment. He thinks at first that the old man is joking. He can't have a hundred dollars to give. But the old man's hands tremble as he reaches into his pocket, producing a wad of bills. He sorts through a hundred, three hundred, too many bills for the boy to count as quickly as they move. The old man draws a rumpled hundred-dollar bill from the wad, holds it up for Caleb to see.

"You don't have to—" Caleb begins to protest, but the old man shakes his head, still holding the bill in front of Caleb's face. There are so many things Caleb could do with that bill. His sister's birthday is next week. She could have a present this time, and a cake. He could take a girl on a date or fill the truck with gas. "Sure, Roland. This weekend." The old man—Roland—shakes his head, shoving the wad of bills back into one pocket, stuffing the bill he's promised to Caleb in the other.

"Now," Roland says, still shaking his head. "Fence, too."

Caleb should be home with his sister now; he'd been on his way inside when Roland had shouted from across the road. Caleb is not brave enough to explain this to the man. Roland keeps shotguns in his trailer. Caleb has heard them go off. Caleb will make this fast. He will make it home by dark, still hours before his father returns from work. So Caleb nods slowly, looking down at Roland's feet, the old man's boots torn and untied around otherwise bare ankles. It's late afternoon already but the sky is thick with curdled clouds. Everything below it is dim.

"Rope," Roland grins around purple gums. He nods toward the little shed just behind the trailer, rubbing at his bare forearm, gesturing for Caleb to follow. Unlike the trailer, the little shed is permanent, built into the ground. The side of the thing is lined haphazardly with old furniture and plywood, tethered to the earth by vines that have grown up around it.

The old man makes his way to the door of the shed, but Caleb stops before. He'll wait outside. Roland turns back, grabs the boy's wrist, tugs. Caleb reels at how entirely he can feel each of the bones in the old man's hand. He fails to step down into the shed, stumbles, but rights himself after a moment. The only light comes from the open door behind the two. As his eyes adjust, he can see the silver spoon that lies in the middle of the dirt floor. Caleb cannot stand up straight for the low ceiling of the shed, heaped to its brim on every side with rusting cans of paint thinner, cardboard boxes loaded with clouded and jaundiced glass, huge warped bottles of antifreeze and ancient cleaners.

Roland turns over his shoulder, flinging a brittle coil of rope toward the boy's face. Caleb reaches out, taking the rope. Roland turns back and continues to rummage. A few moments later he surfaces, having collected a hammer and a mouthful of nails that he clutches between his jaws. Roland smiles and winks at the boy. His face is mangled in the crude half-light, the nails jutting between his lips like the fangs of some unimaginable sea monster that shoves against Caleb's forearm, nudging him back outside.

Back outside, Caleb notices something—music—in the still autumn air. It comes from inside Roland's trailer. There is a light on inside, orange and warm against the gray sky and dinge of the trailer. Someone passes by inside the window, hazy behind the little curtain that covers the bottom half of the glass. Caleb doesn't remember Roland ever having a wife or any person of his own.

"'ay!" Roland calls. Caleb turns to find the old man struggling with the pile of junk against the shed. He grips a two-by-four on the bottommost layer of debris, his hands going white as he yanks up against the rest of the rubble. Hunched over, Roland licks his lips and breathes shallowly, so he has to do it again—too fast. He pants. Caleb sets the hammer and rope down in the moldy grass. He hurries over, pulls the old dresser drawers filled with blue jeans and muck off from on top of the two-by-four. He lays them atop the mud at the corner of the shed and tugs at the moldy board. It snaps away from the vines that anchor it to the ground and Caleb's hands slip against the board's slick surface.

The old man with the sunken face is standing too close to the boy and to the board. The edge of the thing is sharp with its careless cut and the single bent nail that juts out of the board like a broken finger. As the board falls from Caleb's hands, its auburn nail catches the top of Roland's bare arm. The nails Roland still clenches between his jaws tumble to the ground like great shards of broken teeth as he recoils.

"Fucker," he screeches. The sound is high and choked and inhuman. "*Rotten, dirty fucker!*"

Caleb is terrified, frozen to the ground where he stands. He will not be able to take any girl on a date and he will not be able to buy his sister a birthday present. He will certainly not be able to fill the truck with gas enough to get him anywhere. Roland's arm is already drenched with blood. It's begun to seep into the stitches of his clothing, turning his jeans black, turning the grass below a bright crimson. The skin of the old man's arm is flayed down a jagged black line like a fish torn along its belly.

Roland's face contorts with pain and Caleb thinks of the way his mother used to look when she talked about the man she loved before she knew Caleb's father. He thinks of the way her face looked each time she drank a bit too much and shouted at her husband for letting her stay here, for getting her stuck. He thinks of the look on his little sister's face the last time his mother hit her. He thinks of the look on his sister's face after their mother left and didn't come back again.

Caleb moves, reaching for the old man's arm, reaching to staunch the blood or to help somehow. Roland shakes his head furiously, clutching his arm against his own chest, heaving. He turns, trudging back toward the trailer, leaving the boy behind in the yard, the board and its nail lying face-up in the blood-slick grass.

Roland whimpers with each step he takes and disappears into the trailer through a side door the boy hadn't realized was there before. The thing rattles open and when it shuts, Caleb can see the bright smear of blood left above the door's handle. The light inside the trailer is still golden, too bright against the rest of the dimming scene.

Some muffled trail of music still seeps from the trailer. Walls are thin when you can't afford them; Caleb has always known this. Out here where land and air are cheap, sound carries, crystalline. Even on the days when they were sent outside to play, the boy and his sister could hear their mother shriek.

Caleb follows the music toward the little trailer.

He stops midway across the yard when he realizes he cannot hear the song any longer because Roland has begun to shout inside. A woman's voice shouts back.

"Clea' goddamn shit 'fore —"

Something — a pan? — clatters against the floor or the wall or the counter.

"Everything's —"

The music plays, still, beneath it all.

" — wouldn'ta fuckin' left it wi' yer — "

A baby begins to scream, louder, somehow, than either adult.

"Drippin' on the floor, you'll fuckin' knock — "

The sound of a feeble trailer door slamming sounds and the shouting stops. The baby still cries.

Caleb has found his way up the first step into the trailer and the second step too, and the trailer isn't set properly enough that it requires a third step, so Caleb has found the door. He is careful to open it so it makes no noise, or almost no noise, and he presses his way inside.

The air in the trailer smells overwhelmingly of nail polish, the way Caleb's parents' house used to before his mother had left and before she was too much of a drunk to keep her beauty salon in the garage. As Caleb steps slowly inside, he is unsure whether to announce his presence or attempt to back out, unnoticed. But Roland still has his money.

The girl who stands in the kitchen notices Caleb before he can decide for himself how to go on.

The trailer's kitchen is small, but every inch of space is covered — tins of paint thinner like the ones in the shed out back, mason jars duct-taped to endless lengths of kinked garden hose identical to the one the boy's father hooked to a punctured tin can the summers when the boy was young, metal spoons, and unlabeled aerosol cans sprawl across the counter and stove. The baby has stopped screaming, but leans now against the cupboard and whimpers, unnoticed by its mother. The child has no teeth. Its hair still curls freshly against its temples, bright blonde against cheeks flushed from sobbing and from the rash that crawls up its bare ribs and across its face. The person Caleb had seen from outside smiles from beside the stove.

He knows her. Or he knew her, once.

She is blonde and small and much thinner now than she was when the boy knew her. Her eyes have begun to sink, her skin shrinking against the bones of her face. Still, Caleb thinks, she's beautiful. Her name was Dallas, he remembers. Still is, he supposes. The girl was two years ahead of Caleb in school but she left before she was really finished. She's never known Caleb, he doesn't think. Dallas doesn't think she's ever known him either, but she approaches him until she's come too close so their noses nearly touch. She smiles dreamily all the while. Caleb doesn't back away. Steam rises from the stove behind her. Suddenly, Caleb remembers the music that plays, recognizes an old Elvis ballad. He remembers his mother singing, twirling, stoned, around the living room.

"I just need," Caleb clears his throat, looking at the ground, "I need my money. Or if I should leave, I need . . . I need to go." Dallas nods.

"You're awful sweet," she says, as if Caleb hasn't spoken at all. "You look just like this boy I knew once. Handsome. And sweet." Caleb opens his mouth to say something, anything; he can't believe she remembers him. But she keeps talking. "My cousin, Jeremy. He's dead, though." Caleb closes his mouth.

"I'm sorry."

"What for?" Something on the stove begins to shriek like a teakettle, rattling so the baby begins to cry once more. Dallas doesn't seem to notice. Still smiling dreamily, she reaches down and takes Caleb's hand. Dallas squeezes his fingers together so they ache and he sees the spots on her arms where blood vessels have broken, tiny purple fireworks. She doesn't let go of Caleb's hand when the door at the back of the trailer bangs open.

When Roland bursts out of the back room he has a length of paper towel, already drenched scarlet, fastened to his arm with a strip of masking tape on either end, blood pooling against them like water around a gutter. He looks first from Caleb to the stove, then from the stove to Dallas. He never looks at the baby, still screaming, leaning against the oven. Roland begins shaking his head vigorously. "No," he says. "No—no." He limps toward the boy, a growl of sorts rising in his throat. He grabs Caleb roughly by the arm, the way Caleb's mother used to, so there'd be a bruise tomorrow, and if Caleb were still small, his teachers would ask about the marks, and believe him when he lied.

Roland drags the boy along through the trailer, out the door, down the steps, back outside into the day that has become night.

Still, the child screams inside the trailer. The Elvis ballad that played hasn't finished. Somewhere inside, there is the sound of a hearty popping. Somewhere inside is the voice of the girl the boy once knew, as she begins to sing, the beats between her words filled with the sounds of clattering or shattering glass.

"'S grab 'er," Roland spits, shoving Caleb in the direction of the rope and hammer and sprinkling of nails left on the grass. Caleb's heartbeat doesn't slow. It is dark and he ought to leave. For a moment, the boy thinks he hears his mother calling for him from the house across the road, but the house is dark and his mother hasn't been around to call for him in a year, and anyway, Caleb isn't sure he'd be brave enough to leave. He will stay for the money and because Roland has shotguns inside the house. Caleb has heard them go off. He turns, fumbling the coil of rope and hammer from the ground. When he stands, he follows the old man with the gaunt face and arm soaked with blood. Roland carries the board himself this time. He trudges toward the silent pasture of cows.

The window of Roland's trailer is still bright and golden against the purple sky, but as the pair moves farther from the house, Caleb finds that he can no longer hear the music or Dallas's singing from inside. Perhaps she's shut it off.

Roland stops and launches the rubbery board like a javelin over the topmost rail of the fence. He doesn't aim for a cow, but he isn't so careful to aim away, either. One shifts, but doesn't stop grazing. Roland ducks between the middle boards, stringy body looping easily through, though the old man groans as he straightens. The boy trembles where he stands behind the old man, glancing back at the house one last time before quickly ducking through the fence himself. The two pass over flattened grass, down the slight decline of the pasture to the edge of the little lake, fenced off from the field except in the place where one rail is split, the rotten wood lying on the ground.

In the center of the little lake, the cow who'd drowned herself has begun to float.

Caleb looks for a minute out at the murky water. He watches the way the cow's body revolves slightly. He keeps track of her revolutions, bobbing atop the water as a single leg juts skyward.

The old man looks at the boy looking at the cow. Roland reaches out and snatches one end of the rope from the boy. He gestures toward the carcass where it floats in what's surely the deepest part of the lake. As Caleb turns, startled, looking at the old man, Roland gestures again, and this time he tells the boy what to do.

"Go."

On her birthday, Caleb's little sister will be seven. She's received birthday gifts four times in her life. Caleb has never taken a girl on a date, though he's liked one for ages. He's never driven within a hundred miles of the state line. Caleb's father sleeps four hours each morning when he returns from one job and readies himself for the other. Caleb steps into the mud on the shore of the little lake because he's never had a hundred dollars before.

The water is cold with late fall. Its surface is scaly with rotten leaves and cow shit and Caleb's pants turn black the moment he steps in. He sinks up to his elbows in the water and is reminded of the way he feared quicksand so constantly as a child. The old man watches from the pasture at the edge of the lake, clutching his end of the rope, doing little else but trembling there, and mumbling words Caleb cannot or will not make out. Once in a while, Roland glances over his shoulder at the trailer up the hill. Caleb's teeth begin to chatter with cold, so he clenches them together. They ache instead.

Caleb's knee catches the bloated ribcage of the dead animal

that floats in the deepest part of the little lake. She buoys against the water's surface like a child's toy.

The cow's legs are stiff like the old foam pool noodles that rot behind houses. They do not bend at their joints and Caleb realizes he's not sure if they ever did. He wraps the rope between the cow's legs, then around each one again. His hands tremble and he cannot make them stop and he pulls too hard so one leg cracks like a log busted between his hands. Caleb imagines that blood fills the water, but the night is too heavy to tell and the cow is too dead to bleed.

Caleb tugs hard on his end of the rope. He leads the carcass back to shore, his feet suctioning against the floor of the lake with every step, the rope pulling and burning against his frozen hands as Roland gathers the slack at his feet, staring out over the far edge of the pasture and into the woods or the sky above them. Caleb climbs out of the water, tugging at the cow until she bottoms out and the boy is no longer strong enough to pull her along. He drops the rope and looks to Roland. The man's face is yellow and sunken and he nods but does not look at Caleb.

"Don' go lookin' . . . at what yer not s'posed to see." Roland nods as he speaks. Or maybe he's only trembling. Still, he doesn't look at Caleb. "Fence—later."

He turns back toward the edge of the pasture, shuffling over the grass the way they'd come. The old man runs up the hill toward his old blue trailer, greasy with decay. He leaves the boy behind in the pasture; trembling, sopping, dripping onto the already-waterlogged body of the drowned cow.

"*Hey!*" Caleb shouts. "What about my money!" The sound carries in the empty night, but the old man has already flung open the door and disappeared into his rickety old house. Caleb looks at his own feet, at the dead cow and where she lies now, snapped at all her joints, eyes great glass orbs empty and purple like the night.

Then, from the house across the road, a child shrieks. "Caleb!"

So Caleb laces his way back through the parts of the fence that are still intact. He finds his way back down the driveway where the old man had stood an hour before, asking for help. Caleb finds his way to the end of his father's drive where his little sister stands in bare feet, whimpering until she bolts at her brother and flings her arms around his waist. In a few days' time when she is seven years old and she has no present, the little girl will promise she does not mind. She will be thrilled that, this year, she has a cake. She will not know or mind that the mix her brother used to make it was expired.

Caleb will not take a girl on a date. He will tell himself that it's no use anyway; no one marries the girl they date in high school. Not except his father. His father will sleep six hours one night, and it will be by accident, and he will be fired from one of his jobs. When he is, he won't be able to afford the house across the road from Roland's place, and Caleb and his sister will have to pack their things and move to their grandmother's house where they will have to share a bed and their father will sleep on the living room couch.

The boy will not go back to fix Roland's fence. The old man is batshit, and when, after Caleb and his father have moved away, the stove in the old man's trailer finally blows and melts the crying child in the kitchen and the girl the boy knew once and the old man with the sunken face and the teeth like popcorn kernels of black and grease, the hundred dollar bill still tucked away in his pocket, the quiet night sky will be purple and filled with a sound like a gunshot, and there will be no one left to help.

Perhaps the cows will continue to drown themselves in the lake, but the boy will not be around to drag their bodies away.

FALL

We may as well
whirl with leaves
in ice-chipped wind,
spinning, silver maples
no more tethered
to the living, vibrant
rust and amber, pretty
little dying bits —
torn smiles tossed
to wither
through November —
And are we thankful?
for ones who tried,
women and men
with elms in their eyes
poured autumn sun
in raspy laughs,
they gathered words
like golden aster,
flung them free in
lessons taught
with hands, still warm.
Breathing in the splendid
world! Watching
children chewing
macaroni,
their favorite,

before
the bullet holes,
stiff fingers,
noodles cold. Silent
hearts in morning
light beat steady
just   last   night—
bedtime, tiny tears
healthy salt and water,
Mommy, please don't ever die—
In corners, dim
death listened soft
and handed out the guns.

BECOMING WATER

I keep dreaming
I'm turning into water
though I'm unsure
of my form.
I'm decidedly no
tropical sea,
roiling ocean,
or wide river.
I'm neither as lovely
as a raindrop
nor as theatrical
as a waterfall.
I'll settle
for a farm pond
teeming with bass,
ringed with cattails and algae
where occasionally
a woman with shapely legs
cools off.
A doctor friend
assures me
it's a physiologic impossibility,
but I've noticed he keeps
to high ground of me.
We can't dictate terms
to our dreams,
but I'd hate to evaporate.

I fear heights and falling
and adore the earth
too much to leave it.
Let me soak
into the ground
where everything
eventually
comes to rest.

POKING THROUGH THE VOID

How can we believe the water
strider when starlings circle
above the shimmering glass,
or the hare's hunger when
the white owl spreads its wings?
How do we know if we are the dog's
dream or simply a shadow in it?
We will our house toward prayer
when our wanderings should become
our words. We climb the staircase
toward the far field when the lone
sapling that watched over us stands
near. The hour moves, filled with breath
and marrow, and the world ends here.

THE INCONSOLABLE WIND

Sometimes I'm ashamed of the frost
that silvers the grass each morning,
so obvious in its need to conceal.
Or the slow unraveling of moon-bathed
night that trembles to reveal
a kingdom where sight no longer
rules — and the red-eyed raccoons,
and the cries of loons, and the dogs
howling at the — no, not the moon —
at each other. That's really what
this is about, isn't it? The need to cross
between, the mornings we sip tea
made in a far-off country wondering
at every fifteen-cent life left unseen.

"He's going to spoil you," the woman said.

RED BLUFF

At the end of a blistering July, Tessa Dean snuck out of Camp Weyamucca with her best friend Barrett Winslow. It was 1974 and Barrett said they had better things to do than float a canoe across the lake or shoot an arrow at a bull's-eye nailed to a stack of hay. The girls were almost fourteen years old.

The path through the forest was black and cold and smelled of dirty pine needles. Barrett hated the smell and Tessa the dark. They wore Tretorns and tennis socks with little white pompoms attached at the back, above the heel. They had been best friends for three years and went from school to camp together and back to school. They had crushes on different ninth grade boys. Barrett's was blond with green eyes like hers, and Tessa's wore wire-rimmed glasses. She didn't wear glasses, but she was known as studious and careful. She had long, flat dark brown hair and a librarian face, round and neutral, as reported by every mirror she'd looked into hoping for more than the plain nose and almond eyes gazing back at her.

They headed away from the lake toward the road. Barrett held the flashlight, went first. Night was cold in the mountains, the crisp air settled around the lake as if the sun's dry summer heat might never come again. Twigs and pine needles crunched under their steps. Tessa listened hard for bears. Once she heard wings sweeping overhead but she couldn't make out the bird. She wanted it to be an owl. At camp, she and Barrett took their binoculars out at dusk and looked for the owls waking up in the tops of their trees. They had found a mating pair in the spruce trees down by the lake. The male called to the female and then, a minute later, the female called back. They could go for hours like that, the owls, calling back and forth. Tessa and Barrett would sit across from one another, each leaning against a spruce, and make a silent O shape with their mouths, pretending they were the owls.

Tessa thought about turning around. Her pupils felt swollen from the effort of seeing through the softening blackness. The girls still had time to crawl back into their sleeping bags and wake up with the morning revelry, the bells that bristled over the PA system. It was their cabin's turn for sailing, and they were on KP duty, but only at lunch. They had a skit planned for the campfire that night. Tessa and Barrett were playing hummingbirds in a reenactment of a Native American legend. They were going to dive their hands into the air like sharp hummingbird beaks and poke the first stars in the night sky. Tessa reached out to tap Barrett's shoulder, but then she heard the bounce of her friend's backpack, the excitement as Barrett rose up on her toes to take the next step into their journey. Barrett had been planning their trip, she called it, for weeks. As soon as Tessa said all right, Barrett brought out the maps she must've packed from home. She drew dashes in rainbow colors along their route from camp to one little town and then the next. Tessa remembered the maps in Barrett's backpack and let her arm fall back to her side.

When they reached the sign, *Camp Weyamucca – Gem of the California Sierras*, Barrett aimed the flashlight at her hand signal, "Okay." She meant they could speak. They stood along a narrow dirt road.

"Are we doing this?" Tessa said.

"We did it," Barrett said, her eyes glossy in the flashlight's shine.

Barrett could turn five cartwheels across a lawn, one after the other and land on her feet with both arms stretched high above her head like Olga Korbut. Tessa could do only two in a row before her head fuzzed and softened as if it could drift away from her.

"Are you nervous?" Tessa said. She pulled her jacket close

to her sides. She wore it inside out so the Camp Weyamucca seal didn't show.

"Don't be nervous," Barrett said.

"I don't want to be," Tessa said.

Barrett reached for Tessa's hand, and they walked the few miles to town like schoolgirls.

The counselors would search camp first: the cabins, archery range, campfire area, the docks, and swimming raft. And then the boys' camp across the lake. Last summer, three girls from Cabin Perseverance canoed over to the boys' cabins at midnight. They were discovered the next morning, asleep under blankets in a canoe tied to the boys' dock. The camp director sent the girls home. At morning council she lectured the rest of them. She wouldn't stand for canoodling. Barrett and Tessa sat on the splintery pine benches amidst the rows of girls slumped forward in their CW T-shirts. Canoodling in canoes, Barrett whispered, is against the law.

The girls reached the next road, a two-lane strip of asphalt through the middle of the trees. A dull grey dawn turned the pines greenish-black, and waking birds chirped from beneath their cover. The service station soon appeared up ahead; an orange and blue 76 sign tilted on a white pole. Barrett said someone would need gas and stop. Their plan revolved around this gas station.

The 76 sign reminded Tessa of home.

"We're almost there," she said. She fiddled with the teardrop amethyst pendant on the gold chain around her neck. A present from her parents.

If she called her father he'd drive the ten hours from Danville, pick them up in the station wagon straight away, but Barrett had said how they went was as important as leaving. Every few days Tessa's father sent her postcards at camp from the dog. The dog missed her as much as he loved chasing Mrs. Fielsted's orange cat. He made a show of fetching balls and foraging in her mother's petunias as if he didn't. He said the white petunias with the pink stripes tasted like sugar snap peas. Her mother wouldn't let him sleep in Tessa's spot on the couch in the den. Her mother had gone to Weyamucca when she was a girl. She remembered all the songs like it was yesterday. She sent care packages with crumbled molasses cookies and Mad Libs Tessa hadn't played since fourth grade. The same as her mother, Tessa's dead grandmother, had sent when she was a camper.

The gas station had two pumps with rusted handles. Scratched up glass covered the black numbers that rolled up to nine and then back to zero when the gas was flowing. A vending machine leaned against a mechanics garage that attached to a small office. Two panes were cracked in the office window and Tessa considered whether the place had been abandoned. Town wasn't a town, it was the gas station and the post office outlet and a bait and tackle shack further up the road. The camp van had stopped at the shack last summer on the way back from a hike up Mount Shasta. The counselors wanted to use the pay phone. They sent the girls inside for popsicles from the freezer in the back of the bait shop. Half the freezer was stocked with Drumsticks and Bomb Pops and the other with frozen trout, the crystal fish eyes staring as the girls reached in for their treat.

Barrett slotted two quarters through the vending machine and pushed the button for a Coke.

"We'll split," she said.

Tessa wasn't thirsty.

"When do they open?" Tessa said, looking at the dirt and gravel driveways around the pumps and leading into the garage.

"Eight," Barrett said. Though like Tessa, she only knew about the gas station from what she could see. A puddle filled a divot in the gravel between the pumps and the building. The smoky sharp petroleum scent bloomed around them. Tessa's Timex with the Velcro band showed six o'clock.

"You think it'll take till then to get our ride?" Tessa said. She reached for the Coke, drank two big sips. Tessa forgot phone numbers and directions, she scribbled reminders on the back of her hand. Barrett didn't forget, but she liked to decorate their calves with anklets in ballpoint. Sometimes they drew lines of flowers along one another's arms or a secret symbol of the boys they liked above one knee. Glasses for Tessa's crush, and a baseball for Barrett's. Last night as a joke, Barrett had written the address of where they were going — the red star on the map — in permanent marker above Tessa's right hipbone, where no one could see it.

Barrett shrugged and both girls looked up and then down the road.

Headlights approached as if summoned from the direction of Camp Weyamucca. A small red Toyota pickup turned into the gas station and parked alongside the garage. The bottom half of the truck was spattered with mud. A boy got out. He had a crew cut and wore a button down short-sleeved shirt with a 76 on one side and on the other an oval patch that read *Tom*. Barrett and Tessa had stepped behind the vending machine, but he was close enough to read.

The boy straightened the collar of his shirt as if he'd just put it on, tucked a pack of cigarettes in the right sleeve, and then walked around the vending machine to where the girls waited by the garage. He was only a few years older. His pants were worn in the knees and streaked with dried mud, as were the boots he wore with laces loose and frayed. Acne clustered on his cheekbones and his orange hair looked as stiff as straw. He blinked at them slowly, like a toad. His eyes were blue and he had thick pale eyelids.

"You girls are from the camp, aren't you?" he said.

Barrett and Tessa looked at each other.

"You must be confusing us with someone else," Tessa said. She talked to the dim, unattractive boys and Barrett the clever, good looking ones. Barrett had cheekbones and blonde hair and puberty.

"I've worked there, washing dishes in the kitchen," he said.

Tessa nodded like her mother would. Barrett watched the

empty road beyond the boy.

"What are you, runaways?" he said.

"What do you want to know about us for?" Barrett said. She sipped the Coke and then wiped her upper lip with the back of her hand.

Barrett's lips curved into a heart, but the boy didn't look at her any differently than he looked at Tessa.

"I open up the station in the morning and there's you all here and it's my responsibility to know which way this is going," he said. His eyelids opened and closed slow again, saying he didn't care which way it went.

"You don't have reason to think about us," Tessa said. "We'll be gone the first car that comes and takes us."

Barrett elbowed Tessa in the ribs hard enough that Tessa cringed. She turned and caught the gold flints in Barrett's green eyes.

"It's alright, I'm not a talker," the boy said and smiled. He had a split between his front two teeth. "Fact is though, no one's gonna want you."

"We've got money," Barrett said.

"That's good," the boy said. "But you're pretty girls. Could be kidnapping. People traveling around here don't want trouble. They come to get rid of it."

"We just need a ride to meet our parents in Red Bluff," Tessa said.

"How'd you get up here when your parents are down there?" he said. He crossed his arms in front and stood wide like he was daring them.

"Our parents' friends were driving us but their car broke," Tessa said.

The boy tilted his head, as if listening for word from the evergreen branches scratching against the gas station. The wind had come up and the trees swayed.

"Might work," he said.

"When do people start coming in for gas?" Barrett said.

The boy shrugged. He looked up and down the road. Yellow morning light swept over the top of the forest.

"I've been meaning to get down to Red Bluff. My mother's birthday is coming and I want to get her something nice," he said.

They sat three across in the truck, Tessa in the middle. The drive from Red Bluff to camp took five hours on the camp bus from the Safeway parking lot where parents dropped their girls and hugged them goodbye for the month. This morning they were headed south on 85, down from the mountains, and Tom drove fast. He said it would take them four hours, tops. Tessa leaned towards Barrett, but on the curves she couldn't help her leg pushing against Tom's. His thigh felt like one strong muscle. When Tessa and Barrett were alone the few minutes it took Tom to unlock the office and call in sick to his boss, they agreed their plan had worked. "I told you we'd find a ride," Barrett said, but she wasn't preening. By the time he dropped them off and drove back to Weyamucca, if he worked there, they'd be far south. On their way to Hollywood.

They were going to Sunset and Doheny, where Barrett's cousin lived. Barrett's cousin wore knee high boots with sequin miniskirts and worked as a script girl on movies. Barrett visited once and took a picture of her cousin's closet stuffed with silk pantsuits, little sequin dresses, and platform shoes. She swore she was going back as soon as her parents let her, but it had been over a year and her parents said they didn't see the point of Los Angeles. All those freeways and palm trees growing out of dirt squares in the cement. But Barrett didn't care what they thought. She and Tessa would lie on her bed staring at the photograph of her cousin's closet and imagine zipping their legs into shiny white boots.

Tom lit one of his cigarettes, the end burned orange and black. Tessa inhaled the smoke and let the wind from the open windows whip her hair around as they rushed downhill. She forgot the Camp Weyamucca sailboats and her father's station wagon in the heat coming off Tom's leg and the sparkling wardrobe in Barrett's cousin's closet. She felt like she could be in the movies. It was hard to remember that a few hours ago she had wanted to climb back into her sleeping bag. Tom held out his cigarette to Tessa and if she thought she could inhale without choking she'd have taken it. She shook her head. He didn't offer any to Barrett, who was looking out her window into the canyons of skeletal pine trees, their green majesty eaten out by tiny beetles. She seemed sealed up in her world as if they were already on the bus with strangers. She might be thinking about Los Angeles, or the next dotted line on her maps, or a thing Tessa couldn't guess. Tessa liked sitting between Barrett and Tom as if she was the one responsible, the connection, for getting this ride.

They reached the foothills, rolling mounds of scrub brush and short scraggly pines. The highway ran straight towards a vacant horizon as if Red Bluff didn't exist yet. The morning was established now, hot, dry air pouring in through the windows. Tessa wished they'd bought another Coke from the vending machine.

She felt Tom's right foot press down on the gas as he pulled out to pass an RV. Its bumper sticker read, *NO SHIRT, NO SHOES*. Tom laughed.

"That's the life."

The truck swayed left then right as he slid around the RV and back into the lane. Tessa reached out for the dashboard so she wouldn't fall into his lap. There was a rectangular hole with red and black wires sticking out instead of a radio.

"What happened to the radio?" she said. She'd been waiting to ask.

Barrett looked out her window.

"I bought the truck from a guy, radio never worked. I was driving one day and the fuzz was going on it and I threw it out the window. Tore the wires with my teeth."

Tessa felt Barrett's sigh. The teeth were a child's bragging, or he was joking and hadn't got the rhythm. When they were still in the mountains, Barrett had nudged two bottles rolling around the footwell against Tessa's feet. An empty liquor bottle and a full one. The liquor was amber colored and thin as water.

"Why don't you get a new radio?" Barrett said. Tessa was the only one who knew she wanted to be a singer.

"I haven't found the one I want."

Tom opened his palm on the steering wheel. Freckles covered the backs of his hands and ran into the arm of his jacket and then crawled out his collar. If Tessa looked at him from the side, the acne blended with the freckles as if it wasn't there. She had eleven freckles on her nose. The doctor told her mother she'd grow out of them.

"Besides I like the quiet," Tom said. "I hear my thoughts."

"I know what you mean," Tessa said. Barrett elbowed her side and this time Tessa nudged her back. She knew what he meant. She didn't tell Barrett everything that came to her mind. She wondered if Barrett had noticed Tom offer her a cigarette.

"I like music, don't get me wrong. But when I'm driving—" He took a last drag on the cigarette burned down to a stub and threw it out the window. "That bumper sticker on the RV, for example, got me thinking," Tom said.

"About what?" Tessa said. Barrett leaned her head against the passenger window and closed her eyes.

"Usually it's posted on a sign, like in a restaurant: No Shirt, No Shoes, No Service," he said. "Here, they left off the service. They don't want any. They don't care about pleasing. But everybody stands up to the boss, so what?"

He paused and Tessa wondered if she was supposed to answer, but then he went on.

"The part that gets me is the words themselves."

"No shirt, no shoes," Tessa said carefully, as if to learn from it.

"They're *free birds*. You get it?" He looked over, his blue eyes lit up. She wondered what his mouth tasted like. She'd never kissed someone with red hair and that many freckles.

"They're doing whatever they want," she said.

"And wearing what they want. Or maybe nothing. They could be nudists. Driving from one colony to the next, stripped down naked."

Tessa felt her cheeks flare with color. Naked people in an RV. She laughed.

"Is that what they are?"

"I don't know, but I like to *think* they might be," he said. He turned to her again and smiled. The gap in his teeth made his face interesting, his own kind of handsome. "Maybe we should go back and ask them?"

"No!" she said. She covered her mouth with her hands as if shocked or embarrassed, though she wasn't.

"I bet they'd take us to some parties," he said. He checked the mirrors and flicked on his blinker like he was going to turn around.

Tessa touched his shoulder, her fingers on the crease above his bicep.

"No, no! Please!" she said.

He shrugged and grinned and shifted in his seat, clicked off the blinker. "If you say so. But that could've been a good time we missed out on."

They fell back into quiet. Tessa wished for the missing radio, sound to reunite them. She felt Barrett's body beside her, heavy with sleep. She could sleep anywhere.

Tom checked his watch and looked up at the sky as if he'd heard words from it, or a new thought had come down from there and gathered his attention.

Tessa considered the sky, cloudless and still, and where his mind had drifted. When he spoke again she felt hopeful, until she realized his words.

"Why don't you reach down there and see what we've got?"

he said and pointed to the whiskey bottle wedged behind Barrett's Tretorns.

They drove from the foothills into flat, endless acres of dull grasses and sagebrush. Power lines ran alongside the highway, dipping from tower to tower. Tessa sat up straight in the seat and watched each tower grow taller as they sped toward it and then disappear as the truck shot past. Tom steered with one hand at the bottom of the wheel, with the other he balanced the whiskey bottle on his leg, as if this position was common and reliable. For Tessa, it was her first time trying whiskey, or liquor of any kind.

The brown liquid fired down her throat, even when she allowed only a trickle in her mouth. Tom didn't encourage her to drink, but he handed her the bottle and that was enough. He kept the bottle longer on his turns, pointed its neck in the direction of rivers he liked to fish and the lonely tire tracks that led to them. Tessa couldn't make out any distant gullies in the scorched land or pockets of cottonwood trees or other signs of water. Though she imagined him alone on a riverbank at sunset — his favorite time, he said, to fish — casting a rod into a pocket of gurgling river, and then the line catching and him arching back, muscles rippled beneath his shirt as he reeled in a silver trout.

Tessa felt the alcohol zing in her head. She turned older with each sip, her body smooth, pliant, ready. If the radio worked she would turn it loud. Or not. She didn't want Barrett to wake up. Barrett's golden hair had fallen over half her face. She couldn't feel it tickling her cheek, or hear them talking.

"She's a real sleeper," Tom said.

"The car knocks her out. She sleeps the whole way to camp and the whole way back." She caught the word, camp. "I mean the campsite where we go with our parents."

"That's okay," he said.

"That's okay, what?" She spoke softly. She didn't want to sound like a drunken kid. Tom handed her the bottle again and their fingers touched as she took it. His skin was rough. He had working hands. She drank this time for real and barely felt the burn.

"I don't care about your business," he said.

"We're going to Red Bluff to get a bus to Los Angeles. Barrett has a cousin who works in the movies."

"You want to be in the movies?"

She shrugged. Maybe she did. He asked as if her being an actress was a real possibility.

"Barrett likes it there and I've never been and camp was a drag." She handed him the whiskey, the side of her up against him though the highway ran straight as an arrow across the withered fields. When she let go of the bottle, she let her arm brush his leg. She felt they were inches, minutes, from their first kiss. If he didn't have to keep his eyes on the road, if Barrett wasn't on the other side of her.

"I woke up this morning like it was any other day," he said. "And then I meet a girl like you."

They drank half the bottle. Or Tom did, with her help. Then he screwed the cap on tight with one hand, his other balancing the wheel. He didn't want them to get shitfaced, he said. Tessa giggled. She couldn't help it. He told her to put the bottle back careful, so she didn't wake Sleeping Beauty. She slid the bottle beneath Barrett's legs as quiet as a mouse. Tom handed her a stick of gum. He asked her questions: what she liked to do (lie on her bed and listen to records), her favorite color (turquoise), the food she could eat every day and never get tired of. She said milkshakes, which didn't make sense as she'd get sick of milkshakes, but it was hot in the truck and that's what came into her head, liquid thick with cold. He told her about his father leaving when he was ten and his mother working jobs till late at night. Tessa didn't know anyone who'd lost a parent. He said it wasn't like that, his father wasn't dead, just gone. There was a difference.

Barrett woke up as they turned off the freeway and slowed for traffic. She yawned and stretched and stared out at the Red Bluff car dealerships. Tessa and Tom were looking ahead out the window, enjoying the easy silence between them, Tessa thought. She felt like Barrett had slept through months, too long to catch up. She chewed the spearmint gum Tom had given her and waited long enough for Barrett's eyes to adjust to the light shining off the rows of windshields in the parking lots.

"Tom will drop us off at the bus station," Tessa said.

Tom had both freckled hands around the wheel, at ten and two as Tessa's father had taught her.

"It's not far. I've got a stop to make on the way," he said.

Barrett smoothed her hair back into a ponytail and looped a pink elastic band from her wrist around it.

"Where?" she said.

"Tom's picking up that present for his mom," Tessa said. Her tongue was thick with the whiskey. She tried to separate her words.

"Her birthday's the day after tomorrow," Tom said. It was as if they were making up a story. But Tom had a mother, and it was her birthday.

Barrett looked at her and Tessa looked back. She studied the black dots in the center of Barrett's glowing eyes. She twisted her mouth to say, like we have another option. Barrett sighed and turned to her window.

"I'm hungry," Tessa said. She was starving. After the drive with Tom in the truck she sensed she would feel only in extremes. She'd be starving, exhausted, desperate. And she could see things differently. Red Bluff, for example, was uglier than she remembered. Low flat buildings with pipes sticking out the top of them. The dust from the dry, brittle land underneath seeping up over the cement into the desert air. The mid-day sun glazed the storefronts yellow. In the next block, they passed the Safeway parking lot. Cars turned in and out of the driveway; people walked toward the market to buy their gallon of milk. Tessa didn't want to linger here looking for a bus or a ride. What if Tom drove them straight through to LA?

"Get out a sandwich," Barrett said. They'd packed cheese sandwiches from yesterday's lunch.

"Don't feel like it," Tessa said. She wanted a hamburger.

"We'll get food at the station," Barrett said. She pulled her backpack onto her lap, opened and closed pockets confirming their contents.

"You have enough money?" Tom said.

"We have enough," Barrett said.

Tessa had given Barrett the twenty-three dollars she had left of the cash her mother packed her for the camp store. She didn't know how much they had altogether. Or the cost of bus fare to Hollywood. Once she agreed to go, she had trusted Barrett. It was her idea, her cousin, her maps that would get them through.

"To go all the way to Los Angeles?" Tom said.

"Who said we were going there?" Barrett said. But she didn't elbow Tessa. She held the backpack and looked ahead out the window.

Tom ducked and peered out at the stores as if he were checking addresses or hoping for a certain place to identify itself.

"I heard it around," he said.

"He guessed," Tessa said, like she had no part in it. "He won't tell." Hunger drew her stomach into an ache. Her leg rested against Tom's as if it had come that way, heavy and unmovable and dependent. On her other side, Barrett had shifted towards the door. There were inches of vinyl seat between them.

"I mind myself," Tom said.

Barrett had her hand on the door handle. Her other hand on her backpack.

"Let us out."

"Barrett, it's fine. Relax," Tessa said, her tongue rolling over in her mouth.

"Let us out, now," Barrett said.

Tom drove on as if she'd said nothing.

"Barrett, calm down, we're going to stop at this store and then we'll go to the bus," Tessa said.

Barrett looked at her, studied her eyes but Tessa knew they wouldn't give way. Her eyes were wide open. She could see the line indented on Barrett's cheek from sleeping against the side of the truck.

"We don't have time," Barrett said.

"We have all the time," Tessa said. It was her trip as much as Barrett's.

"That doesn't make sense, you're not making sense."

"Because I'm not doing what you want?"

"What are you talking about?"

Tom slowed at the curb, in front of a jewelry store.

"Here we are," he said. He leaned forward and looked at them. Tessa watched his eyes slide from Barrett's face down her long neck and over her chest before he turned to Tessa.

"You're gonna help me pick something out, right?" he said. And then to Barrett, "She's got that pretty necklace. I could use her advice."

Tessa touched the amethyst on her chain, felt for the tiny diamonds around her birthstone.

Barrett sat up in her seat and tightened her ponytail.

"There's always a woman in these stores and she'll have advice for you," Barrett said. "We've got to get to the station."

Tom reached over Tessa and opened the glove box in front of Barrett. He smelled like cigarettes and gasoline and whisky. He pulled out a baseball cap, knocked the glove box shut and slid the hat on his head.

"It'll only take a minute," he said.

"We've got to go," Barrett said, her lips pursed together. Tessa could barely see the heart in them.

"Only a minute," Tessa said, bargaining with her endless time.

She wanted to look at necklaces with Tom. More than she wanted to go to Los Angeles, more than she wanted anything.

"Then I'll take you girls to catch your bus to Hollywood," Tom said.

"I don't think it's a good idea," Barrett said quietly, just for Tessa.

"I don't mind," Tessa said.

She smiled at Barrett as if she were helping the three of them out, doing this one favor.

Tom got out and Tessa slid across his seat into the street. She followed him around the front of the truck and held up her finger to show Barrett she'd take a minute and not any more. Barrett stared from behind the windshield and shook her head.

The store was air-conditioned. A glass counter ran along each side and another across the back. An older woman stood at the back counter polishing a watch. Permed ash blonde ringlets clung around her pale face. Her cheeks were shiny, or oily, like she'd put on Vaseline instead of make up. Over her eyes, she'd penciled brown eyebrows with sharp peaks.

"Good morning, ma'am," Tom said.

The woman smiled. "Good morning," she said, and the eyebrows climbed her forehead. On her wrist she wore a plastic yellow coil bunched with small keys.

"I brought my girlfriend to help find a necklace for my momma's birthday," Tom said. He put his arm around Tessa, drew her shoulder snug under his armpit. A lightness burst down her arms and legs, into her toes. She'd never been held and owned.

"She's lovely." The woman's brown eyes were moist and receding. Her arm tittered with a mild tremor and the keys around her wrist bounced faintly on the glass counter.

When Tom spoke again, his voice boomed above the whir of the air conditioner mounted in the window behind the woman.

"We'd like to look at your gold necklaces," Tom said.

The woman picked through her keys and then slid them

into locks and opened the sliding panels on two of the cases. She reached in for the necklaces dangling on velvet stands. She pulled one out and then another and another, arranged them on top of the glass.

Tom leaned forward to examine the gold chains. Some had round links and others S-shapes that fit right together as if they'd been glued. Each chain had a pendant. There were open gold hearts, circles of diamonds, and blue sapphire stars. Tessa didn't see any amethysts.

"Momma loves diamonds," Tom said.

"I've never met a woman who doesn't," the woman said. "My favorite are the initials. Pave they call it. It's the style of setting those little diamonds close together."

"Do you have a D for Doreen?" Tom said. A gold chain with a diamond D hung from the third necklace stand on the counter. Tom could see it as well as Tessa.

He watched the woman peer down into the cases and then pause above the one case she hadn't opened yet. It held what Tessa's mom would call fine jewelry: engagement rings, bracelets, earrings, and necklaces glittering with diamonds under the store lights. The diamonds were large and white. When the woman moved past the expensive jewelry and back towards Tessa and Tom, Tessa heard Tom's breath going in hard and then coming out fast like he was angry. The woman examined the displays she'd already set in front of them and found the D.

"Here it is," she said. Tom smiled as if he were grateful and took the necklace. He held it out in front of Tessa like you would a sweater to see if it was the right size.

"It's nice," Tessa said, as his girlfriend in the jewelry store.

"You didn't need her help after all," the woman said.

"Moral support," Tom said and drew Tessa to him again so they admired the necklace dangling from his hand together. She caught the tang of his odor and felt dampness under his arm.

He set the D necklace back on its stand and pointed at another, in the case with all the diamonds.

"I'd like to see my girl wearing that one," he said. "Can we try it?"

The three of them looked down through the glass. Tom had chosen a necklace made only of diamonds, one after the other building in size from either side until they met in the middle around one giant sparkling jewel, as if designed for a princess.

"He's going to spoil you," the woman said. She unlocked the glass case and set the necklace on the counter.

Tom lifted the diamonds from the velvet and opened the clasp. He moved behind Tessa and rested the cold stones on her skin. She gathered her hair and held it up for him. His fingers glanced the back of her neck and she shivered. When he finished, the woman crossed her hands over her heart.

"Dear, look in the mirror," the woman said to Tessa, "It's breathtaking."

Tessa turned to the framed mirror on the counter. She looked like she was playing dress up with her mother's jewelry box. That is if her mother had owned fancy jewelry. But when she looked up from the necklace to her straight lips and her freckled nose and her almond eyes, she could no longer see the librarian. She hesitated on her features, where they had altered, when Tom spoke.

"We'd better get going," he said.

"I can wrap your gift real nice," the woman said. She picked up the necklace for Tom's mother and hurried through the door in the back of the store.

Tom reached in his back pocket and shook out a crumpled plastic bag.

"You be quiet now," he said to Tessa.

He walked behind the glass counters and tried the sliding doors. He smiled when they opened. The woman had left them unlocked, every one, as he'd intended. He started with the diamonds, reached in and grabbed at the rings and watches and bracelets and necklaces. Then he shook out the velvet displays left on the counter. The necklaces dropped into the bag like worthless candy.

Tessa watched Tom. He rushed to the next cases as the air turned thick and balled up around her like cotton.

"She's slow as shit, but she'll be back and we'd better be gone. You wanna help me?"

The air conditioner shuddered to a stop. Tessa didn't know if he'd asked her a real question. If he expected her to bend down beside him and reach under the display lights and swipe at the hoop earrings and little ring stands. She'd never work as fast with him as he could alone. Tom cleared the last case and turned at the door, his plastic bag swinging from one fist. He glared as if she were a child who had disobeyed. She was meant to follow him.

"You're not good for much," he said. He grabbed her arm and led her out the door into the white daylight. She winced at the brightness. She felt him guide her into the street, around the truck. She heard the door open and then he shoved her inside and climbed in after her. He started the truck and they jerked away from the curb, into the passing traffic.

When Tessa's eyes opened she realized that she had not thought about Barrett once, and then, that Barrett wasn't in the truck.

"Looks like she abandoned you," Tom said. He yanked the buttons off his shirt with the "Tom" on it, shrugged it from his shoulders and dropped the shirt out his open window. He had a grey T-shirt on underneath. She'd never noticed.

"My name's Mark," he said.

Barrett and Tessa had decided that if they were split up, they would meet at the apartment. She had the address in black ink above her hip. *1125 Doheny Drive.*

Tessa slid over to Barrett's side of the truck. She didn't know about the real Tom, if he was tied up in a ditch or searching his dresser for his missing 76 shirt and keys. Or if Mark was the real Tom turning over another leaf. She wouldn't need an alias for robbing the jewelry store. Had she robbed it? The necklace sat heavy on her chest. The woman in the store didn't know her name, of course, just what she looked like.

"You can't count on girls like that," he said. "They can't help it. They've had too many advantages."

Tessa imagined Barrett leaving the truck and walking alone down the sidewalk, away from the jewelry store. When she tried to see Barrett's face, what she was thinking, Barrett wasn't Barrett anymore. It worked better if Tessa watched a stranger come and take Barrett from the truck and she was slapping and kicking him but he was big and strong and no one came to stop him. Tessa wouldn't know unless she got to Hollywood and found out whether Barrett was there, or not. But she didn't have any money, only a princess's necklace.

Tom kept checking the rearview mirror and out the side windows.

"I'm sorry about what I said in the store. You played your part better than if I'd told you what to do," he said. "I get hot in the head when it's time to go, don't mean anything by it. Adrenaline."

His eyes ran over her as they had on Barrett, her face, her neck, her chest.

"You look real pretty in that necklace," he said.

Tessa's hand went to the necklace, its hard, cut stones. In the windshield she could see the diamonds reflected, flinty in the sunlight.

"Take it off now," he said.

She reached behind her neck and tried for the clasp. There were two parts, a latch to unhook and then a button to push that released the necklace. Her fingernails were too short to lift the latch but she kept trying, while he rapped a thumb against the steering wheel.

"That's all right," he said. "Let's try this." He lifted the neck of her T-shirt, his fingers soft on her collarbone, and tucked the shirt up and around the diamonds.

The covered necklace pressed into her.

"You want to eat? We'll drive a little ways, there's a place that has the best milkshakes I ever tasted. My Daddy used to take me there, before he left, when I was a kid. I didn't ask which flavor you like, vanilla or chocolate?" Tom said.

Tessa searched the sidewalks for Barrett with her backpack slung over her shoulders. The up and down glide of her steps, her backpack floating behind her. Tessa slipped her fingers inside the waist of her jeans, but she couldn't feel Barrett's handwriting on her skin. She wondered if later a stranger would find the address on her body and believe it could solve a crime.

The boy was watching her now, his blue eyes fierce on her.

"What flavor you like?" he said.

The sun bore down on the stucco buildings, on the squinting cars ahead. The glare reached into the truck and spread over Tessa until she breathed the stale heat and it coated her lungs with invisible dust. She looked out the window for the bus station or Barrett or a police car or a sign to follow back to where she had started that morning, alone in the trees with her best friend, walking through the dark.

WALK WITH MY FRIEND

Ahead of me, my friend turns to wave,
continues his long-legged stride on the trail
while I dawdle over last blooms of autumn flowers.
At the river's overlook, we catch-up, spot a heron,
but no high, circling ospreys. I miss their calls,
remark, *It seems early for their southern exodus.*

He nods in silence to my chatter, words trapped
in his brain's errant pathways. If he could
would he comment on the ospreys,
the late blossoms? Are his thoughts
a bee fussing on the wrong side of the screen,
or the warmth of an old flannel shirt?

On camping trips, years ago,
with all of our children
thumping around us,
he and I would perch on camp stools,
drink coffee, debate the merits of basketball
for our first grade girls.

Back at his house,
he pauses to hear my count
of the miles we covered.
More muscle next time, I say,
and he smiles, aware
of who is the straggler.

His wife asks, *Are these walks a burden?*
No, no, I say, gripped by the courage
each of them must gather each day. She bends,
plunges her gardener's hands into fresh soil,
potting her porch planters with spring flowers
that won't survive an early frost.

HORIZON

Already tall at twelve, Anna clambers up the ladder,
impatiently peels the adhesive loose, reaches
her strong arms to place the plastic stars
across the ceiling in random order.

She has painted the walls of her room
a deep evening blue and we gather
with lights off to admire
the first flickers of the starry night.

Now grown and launched
on her own trajectory, she speeds
towards the maze of Hubble's images
while I am caught here at the horizon.

I slip between her flannel sheets
switch off the light and wait
for the stars to emerge.

EVE COMES CLEAN ON THE SUBJECT OF TEMPTING ADAM

Story goes: under the dawn-devouring canopy she had to bite
her tongue at a father-God, thinking to herself, Why *that* tree?

She had hoped for better than a first hissee fit. Instead of love,
he was giving her the divine what-for for such a simple thing.

If she did what they say, which was to tempt a weaker Other,
deporting herself like she had just stepped out of a Lana Del

Rey song where the singer is walking off the hum after sex—
I know: this is before Song. But if she did what they say,

so what? Nothing was anything. Everything at its start.
And so what she did is outside the constraints of morality.

Still, she and Adam had to pay up. Facts around the first
death they witnessed must've knocked them over as Eve

wondered what sort of truly beautiful movie ends like that,
the audience asking itself what the fuck that was all about.

I sat in the traffic jam . . . listening to the soft sounds
of Yiruma's piano attempting to erase the rain.

WINGS

When I was four, my family and I took a trip to the Bahamas. This is the earliest memory I have of a migraine.

"I bet it's the flying," I overheard my mom say. "I bet it's the pressure from takeoff and landing." My dad nodded.

When we arrived at the hotel, I tried to articulate the pain. But with a limited, four-year-old vocabulary, I didn't quite know how to explain that the room's white walls were hurting my eyes; that I needed the hot breeze to stop blowing the wind chime out on the front balcony; that I needed the floor-to-ceiling curtains to stop dancing, to stop casting shadows and sharp glares around the room.

"You're not used to the flying, Sweetiepoo," my mom insisted. "Your ears just need to pop. Lie down for a bit and I'm sure you'll feel better."

I buried myself under the covers, blocking out the bright Bahamas sun. I used the palm of my hand to apply pressure to my left eye and temple.

A little while later, my head was still hurting. My mother drew back the covers and handed me a piece of gum. "Why don't you try chewing this for a few minutes? Sometimes a piece of gum helps."

I placed the pink rectangle in my mouth. Suddenly, the fruity smell was in my nose, the sugary taste on my tongue, the candy dye sliding down my throat. It seemed as if the pain had doubled, tripled, in a matter of seconds. I started to scream, started to slap my face. And then I threw up.

I don't remember anything else after that.

More often than not, I have no idea that a migraine is on its way until it has arrived. These are the moments when I am so mortified by my inability to control my own body's actions that I am almost able to forget about the pain.

Almost.

Like in ninth grade math, sitting in silence with the rest of the class, trying to solve for X. But then there was pain in my left eye, concentrated and searing. My pencil dropped from my hand and suddenly I was face down on the floor.

Girls crowded around me, offering tissues and cups of water. For a moment, I was embarrassed, ashamed enough to shift my focus from the pain to my very-wounded pride. But then I couldn't think anymore and I was turning to my side, curling up on the floor, applying pressure to the left hemisphere of my face. Too drained to feel anything but the syncopated, steady throbbing of the migraine.

My mother received a call from the school secretary, and ten minutes later, she burst through the doors.

"Where is she?"

Without a word, the secretary pointed to the assistant principal's office; I was curled in a fetal position on the far right corner of the floor.

"Do you know if she's taken her medicine yet?"

The secretary shook her head.

My mother walked over to me and leaned down. I could hear her breathing hard, still out of breath after rushing through the lobby. She wrapped my arm around her waist and pulled me up slowly. All of the usual school sounds thundered around us: books being dropped and lockers slamming; the bell signaling the start of class; dozens of girls laughing and chattering as they made their way down the hall. I thought my head might explode.

Kids lingered in the lobby, and I could feel their eyes on me as my mother helped me out of the office. But I was too tired to care, too exhausted from the pain and nausea. I rested my head on her shoulder and closed my eyes.

We walked out into the sun, and she lifted a hand to shield my face. "Almost there, honey," she whispered. "The car is just down the block."

Moments later, she carefully helped me into the SUV, leaning the passenger seat all the way back. Then she sped off, never once using the turn signal for fear that the clicking might make my pain even worse.

All afternoon, my mother zoomed in and out of my room.

Are you nauseous? Can I get you some water?

I can make you a sandwich. Are you hungry?

Do you need notes from the classes you missed?

I shook my head. What I needed was to be left alone, to be given space to breathe. But I didn't think my mom knew how to do that.

So I told her I simply needed a nap.

Give them roots but give them wings, I've heard people say. Make sure your children know that they can depend on you, but give them enough independence to explore the world on their own.

When I think of my childhood and adolescence, I do not think of exploration or freedom. I think of my mother, hovering over me, always nearby in case of a migraine attack. And when my memory flashes back to the Bahamas, I think of my mother too. I wonder what it must have been like for her, the pain she must have endured while watching her four-year-old suffer, emotions compounded by the knowledge that if her little girl was, in fact, beginning to get migraines, she had most likely inherited them from her mommy.

I have only asked my mother about this migraine episode once — a few years ago when I began writing this essay — and she refused to talk about anything other than the technical details: the plane ride, the hotel room, the bubblegum.

"What should I tell you, honey? We got through it. I was just so thankful that we got through it, and then I never wanted to think about it again."

She does not permit herself to dwell on these moments and feelings. But I do. I force myself to think of them, to speculate and wonder and guess. Because it is as close as I will ever come to piecing this memory together. And because these are also the thoughts that allow me to see my mother more clearly, to understand her reasons for mothering me the way she did.

Give them roots but give them wings.

These are the thoughts that allow me to realize that wings were never even an option.

By the time sophomore year of high school rolled around, I had seen three different neurologists and had tried over a dozen prescription drugs, none of which had been particularly effective.

Neurologist #4 suggested that I learn to use Imitrex injections. But I refused. The pinch of the metal syringe scared me more than the hours of migraine pain. It was an irrational fear, I knew. But I couldn't seem to help it. I was terrified.

And then I was put into a back-brace for a curvature in my spine, a condition known as scoliosis. I was required to wear the heavy plastic for twenty-three hours a day, and because I was frequently dehydrated, overheated, and sleep-deprived, my migraine condition worsened. Migraines that had typically surfaced two or three times a week were now showing up almost every day. So when my mom brought me home from school one afternoon because of an especially severe migraine, she begged me to allow her to give me a shot.

"*No!*" I shrieked. I ran up the stairs and locked my bedroom door. I sat down on the floor, my knees pulled up to my chest as far as the brace would allow. In the hallway, I heard my mom sit down on the other side of the door.

"Please, honey. Just a few seconds, and it'll be over. You can rest after — "

"Stop talking! *Nooo!*"

My throat was raw from the screaming and sobbing, and I can still call to mind the sound I made, something not quite human. Something reminiscent of grief and mourning.

I sat on the floor, my reflection staring back at me from the mirror: my body trying to fold into a fetal position despite the back brace; sweat dripping down my forehead and neck, disappearing under my shirt; my hand over my eyes, trying to block out the light.

And the tears. I'm not sure whether I was crying because the idea of a needle scared me so badly, or because I was angry at myself for being scared of the needle, or because I was scared that all of this — the migraine pain, the back brace, the lack of space and privacy — wouldn't ever go away. Either way, I cried. Cried myself to sleep. And when I woke up a couple of hours later, I found myself face down on a patch of carpet that was wet from sweat, snot, and tears.

But the migraine was gone.

Soon after that episode, I learned how to give myself injections.

I was seventeen and home by myself. I'd been in bed with a migraine for over an hour, and there was so much schoolwork, so much studying, that needed to get done. I called my mother's cell phone, but she was out running errands. She sounded panicky and said she'd come straight home.

I didn't think I could wait, so I dragged myself down to the kitchen where I knew my mom kept the injections. I stood there with my pajama pants puddled around my ankles, holding an alcohol swab against my thigh.

I counted to twenty — about three or four times — and then pressed the needle to my skin.

I still remember the feeling, the incredible sense of triumph.

It was the first real step I'd taken toward any kind of independence. And when my mother rushed into my dark bedroom twenty minutes later saying, *I'm here, I'm here, let me do it*, it felt damn good answering, *Already done.*

It rained every single Tuesday during my first semester in grad school.

Typically, the showers would let up a bit while I sat through classes. But then evening would settle in, and as eight thirty approached, the rain could be heard, once again, drumming against our classroom windows. By the time I'd reach the parking lot, thunder would be throbbing, veins of water rushing, gurgling, in little streams between parked cars, the rivulets growing bigger and wider and faster as the storm brewed on.

Heavy flooding on the Grand Central Parkway was not unusual. In fact, on one particular Tuesday night in November, traffic updates reported floods on all the major New York highways.

As I signaled and turned onto the ramp, I could see a construction sign in the distance warning of heavy delays, the result of a thunderstorm and a three-to-one lane merge. Dozens of brake lights flashed on and off as the traffic began to bottleneck. As my car crept forward, I felt the familiar pulsing, the throbbing by my left temple which slowly started to make its way toward the center of my left eye.

No, not now. Please not now.

Suddenly, there was honking and a car was cutting into my lane and I was trying to focus but the pounding in my eye had synchronized with the rainwater pounding on my windshield.

Thud! Thud! Thud!

Rain splattered hard against the window. The back and forth of the windshield wipers was unbearable, the side-to-side motions making me dizzy. I had no choice but to turn the wipers off.

There was nowhere to pull over, no shoulder or exit lane. My schoolbag — with my Imitrex injection — sat in the backseat, and I was too scared and too queasy to unbuckle and reach behind for it. So I did the only thing I could think of: I put on some music.

I sat in the traffic jam with one hand over my eye and the other hand on the wheel, barely moving at all, listening to the soft sounds of Yiruma's piano attempting to erase the rain. I listened, all the way home, with tears streaming down my face.

The rest of that night is a bit fuzzy for me. I seem to remember little, unimportant details. Like fumbling for the key outside my house, my hand shaking as I inserted it into the lock. Like pushing past my mom without answering her *Hi honey, how was class?* Like dropping my schoolbag on the stairs while stumbling up to my room.

Everything about that night is black. Sort of like my room, after I turned out the light, curled up in bed, and pulled the blanket over my face.

I like telling myself that I haven't allowed migraines to interfere with my life. It makes me feel strong and confident, proud of the obstacles I have overcome. After all, I am not afraid of pain; I am only afraid of its timing.

The truth, though, is that I have simply traded one fear for another. These days, I find myself afraid of needing help, of accepting help, of depending on anyone at all. I am afraid of returning to the way I was. These days, I fly around, wings spread wide, afraid to come back down to earth.

OLD HOMESTEAD

Bad luck house, when Atlantic waves lashed
your cliff, your picture windows gaped at their power,
and your pretensions flew off like loose shingles
in a blizzard. But the winds always

blew your airs back to you. You gathered them in,
went back to preening your white columns,
your slate roof, your rose granite garden walls,
attracting crows with all your shattered mirrors.

We girls hid in the basement, nursing
our welts and bruises, plotting escapes to the outside.
Waves rolled in and out of your broken cove, pushing
stones and pebbles into sloping dunes.

Looking back, we counted your bad luck hours.
Before our time, the father of the house died in his bath.
Ours went to prison. The next one, too, while his wife
died slowly behind your columns, glass, and granite. Cancer.

She'd been kind when coming to take over.
"It must be sad," she said to the child I was.
"This is your house, too." Not mine, I knew.
"It's nice outside," I hinted, fearing you would wall her in

to hear your slates gloat. I wanted her to listen
to the insects singing down the street, their ten thousand
generations in the marsh behind the stone and pebble dunes.
But now they're gone. The new storms breach every boundary.

LOVE LETTER TO MY INSECURITY

I am sitting
in a strange room
in a town that is not
a bit known to me and
you keep popping in
my head and I know you're
thinking of me, too because
we have always been
close, slept thousands
of toss-and-turn nights
in the same bed
together.

You have told me,
in so many of
our conversations over
the years, that you want
to be held
and I want you
to know I do want
to put my arms
around your scratched
and slivered longing,
but I want you
to also know, as tough
as it may be to hear,
that there is no holding

that can be found on any planet
strong enough
to squeeze you into
a perfection.

You, my darling, are always
going to be close
to me and this I accept
and do embrace you,
love you,
the best I can,
just as a wary-eyed
doe stands still
in an open meadow, allows
her fawn to suckle,
then walks on
knowing it will follow.

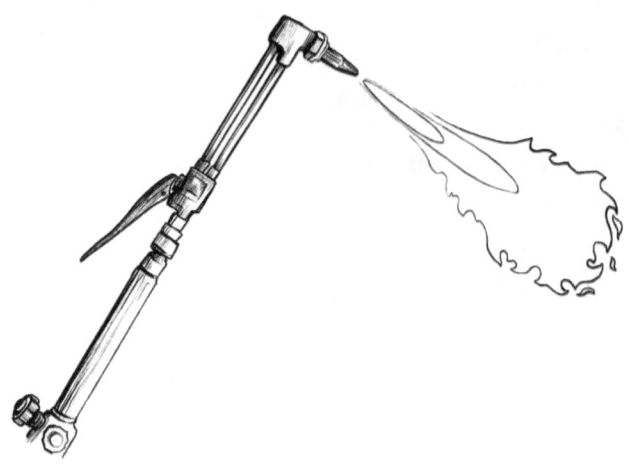

"What's to know? You turn this knob here, this knob here,
light it with a flint striker, and you're off and running."

THE WORKSHOP

Mitch is out in his workshop again, our former dilapidated one-car garage, repurposed. I'd like to just get myself and the kids in the Subaru and shove off, but he would complain about that later. He treats every outing like it's a two-year whaling voyage in the 1800s. We must say goodbye. I'm careful not to look through the garage door windows. Some things can't be unseen, I know. Take it from a woman who once had the misfortune of seeing Mr. Nibbles—no shit, Mr. Nibbles—the second-grade class gerbil devouring his litter of six. What would be the equivalent in this situation? Mitch crying? Mitch just sitting there staring at a wall? Mitch with a blowtorch to his head?

"We're off to my mom's," I say when he answers my knock. He kisses me on the cheek like I'm his sister or have some sort of infectious disease. "Drive safe," he says. "Text me when you get there." He waves to Audrey and Ezra, who are already strapped into their seats. They wave back. Hard to tell what they're thinking. Kids can be amazingly difficult to read sometimes.

It's a two hour drive up to Canton but the kids are used to the trip. They've got their snacks, their workbooks and books. Audrey, who has recently turned eight, has her favorite doll—the trashy one who looks like she has more indulgent parents—and Ezra, who will be five next month, has his stick. No video games or movies for this family. Nope. We old-school it. This is mostly just the result of a tight budget, but Mitch and I have adopted it with pride. Audrey chafes a little under the strictures, savvy enough to understand what she's missing out on. For Ezra's part, he couldn't care less. Even if you gave him an iPad, he'd still end up playing with sticks and rocks instead. I know this doesn't bode well for his cognitive prospects, but Mitch thinks that it might be an indication of his genius. It's not like I'm ready to throw in the towel on the little man, not at all. He's a sweet kid, and sensitive and loving, and in my opinion not half as squirrely as most of the kids in his class. Still, I'm lining up his IEP.

As a parent you can't help but wonder when you look at your kids if they are going to make it in this world. I'm not at all worried about Audrey; she's got the smarts, the independence, the boldness, and the stomach for life. You can't underestimate the importance of stomach. I mean, just last March, her class took that field trip to the meat-packing plant. (Yes, it turns out the teacher, Mrs. Bradley, is a card-carrying member of PETA, and yes, we parents should have been paying better attention to permission slips being shoved under our noses, but it really had been a looooong winter and those of us who weren't on the verge of nervous collapse due to seasonal affective disorder were just glad to see that the kids would be getting out and doing something. And besides, the place had a benign enough sounding name—Green Valley Foods, or something.) At any rate, almost all the kids came back somewhat traumatized and born-again vegetarians, but not Audrey. In trying to talk to her about it using the guidelines the school sent out to all the parents along with sincere apologies and stern reminders that permission slips existed for a reason, blah, blah, blah, I didn't read the whole thing, she said to me, "How did they think the chicken nuggets were made?" How indeed?

But Ezra? I don't like to say it, but he might have too much of his daddy in him.

I wish Nora hadn't already strapped the kids into the car when she knocked on the door. It would have been nice to get some hugs before they left. And what's the matter with that? It's not as if anybody ever sat across from a psychotherapist and said,

"My father hugged me too much as a child." And, sure, we get into our cars and drive off some place almost every day, but that doesn't mean that we'll necessarily come back.

The day my father never came back was my fourth birthday. I awoke to the sounds of my parents fighting, which was how I often woke up on the days my father didn't leave for work at 5 a.m. After a while, I heard the front door slam and I went to my window to look out. I saw my dad climb into the truck of his welder buddy from work. It idled for a few minutes in the driveway, and I thought that maybe they were just talking. It was January and one of those hard, cold, clear mornings that burns your nostrils. But then the truck drove off with my dad still in it. I came downstairs to find Mom smoking in the kitchen, standing in front of the stove as if she were cooking breakfast, but there wasn't anything on the stove to cook. Where did Dad go with Tim? I asked. She said, Daddy went to go get you a birthday cake, hon. Do you want cloud eggs or sunshine eggs? — which was our way of saying scrambled or fried. I thought that it was odd that Dad had gone with Tim to get my birthday cake. It didn't seem likely that Tim had wanted to help pick out my cake, since he'd never seemed to like me all that much: he always called me pipsqueak and punched me on the arm so hard that it would be sore the next day. Did I know that I would never see my dad again? I guess not. I had cloud eggs for breakfast.

I look at the pile of scrap metal in front of me and let my eyes go soft trying to see something in it. What would Ezra see? A secret world, a map of the universe, answers to life's greatest riddles? I'm not sure what he sees when he stares at a rock or a tree so intently, but I'm sure he sees something. Nora thinks he's delayed, but I think he's just special. In this day and age, isn't being content with the simple, as opposed to always wanting more, bigger, better somewhat akin to a magical power? The rest of us live off discontentment like it's food.

I hate to think of him spending the whole day with Nora's

stepfather, Larry. Larry says that the problem with my generation is that we never had a buddy die in our arms. *You've never had warm blood on your hands or looked death in the face and walked away,* he says. *When you've seen the kind of shit I saw over in 'Nam, then you know what it's like to live, and you know what it's like to die, and you know that everything in between is just bullshit.*

Here's the thing: I'm a believer in Karma, and I try not to think bad about people, but Larry is the sort of person whom it's hard not to think bad about. It's almost as if he wants you to dislike him. Maybe he just reminds me a little of Tim. Maybe he just reminds me a little of my father.

Christ. Larry's Mustang is in the driveway. Usually when we come up for these visits he's off golfing or bowling or shooting. Here's the thing: Yes, Larry makes my mother—for whatever completely unidentifiable reason—happy, and yes, he is almost solely responsible for pulling her out of her depression after Dad passed away, for which I will always owe him a sincere debt of gratitude, but Jesus, what a stuff-shirted prick. I can almost hear Audrey's eyes rolling in her head when we pull up next to his car, which I make sure to park at least five feet away from, but Ezra, bless his tiny heart, actually says, "Pop-pop!" with a naked excitement in his voice. To be fair, Larry does seem to have an affinity for Ezra as well. He thinks we molly-coddle him and sees all of Ezra's sticks and rocks not as indicators of cognitive deficiencies or beacons of shining genius, but as a sign of Ezra's deep inner manliness, which he, Larry William Cockburn, Jr., as the most masculine person in Ezra's life, is thereby tasked with nurturing and bringing forth.

My mother still lives in the same house where I grew up—a 1950s ranch that hasn't seen a new coat of paint or stick of furniture since 1975. The walls that aren't orange are paneled in wood, except the one in the living room that is completely mirrored. All the fixtures are shiny brass and the carpets are mustard yellow shag. Despite myself, walking into this house still feels like coming home. The one room that's different from how it was when I lived here is the downstairs den, which Larry has undertaken to outfit like the inside of a taxidermist's showroom. Deer heads, wild turkeys, ducks, angry-looking raccoons, a couple of pheasants, and one armadillo — bagged on a trip to Florida — line the walls and stand in the place of furniture. The coffee table is actually made of two raccoons holding up a glass table top. Everyone but Larry avoids this room, except Ezra, who imagines it as a forest teaming with his wild animal friends. It is to this room that Ezra immediately runs when we enter the house. The Morgue, Audrey calls it. To Ezra, it's Eden.

Mom is in the kitchen, as usual, chopping onions and wiping her tears on a well-used pink tissue. I imagine her as a giant sequoia, at once indomitable and fragile, with an inner core of rings that would tell the story of her life — which years were rainy, which years were sunny, which years were dry, and which years were ravaged by fire and earthquake.

"What's for lunch?" I ask.

"Chili. Do the kids eat chili?"

Do the kids eat chili. Of course the kids don't eat chili. The kids eat chicken nuggets and macaroni and cheese and treat all other food like it might be contaminated with Anthrax. "That's fine," I say. Thankfully, Audrey is already out of earshot in the living room, setting up her basket weaving loom or whatever it is.

My mother's ancient gray cat, whom she calls Prissy but the rest of the family has dubbed Hissy, is busy preening herself on the only kitchen stool not occupied by knitting projects or hunting magazines. When I walk over to the chair, the cat gives me a look that a witch might use to curse one's family for generations, then hisses loudly and bolts off the chair and through the cat flap on the patio door. She disappears into the clump of trees that separates my parents' house from the nearby trailer park, which everyone refers to as The Woods, like it might be the incarnation of some fairytale forest of ancient oaks and majestic evergreens instead of the scrubby collection of honeysuckle and dying ash trees that it is. I see Ezra and Larry out there, too, vanishing into the underbrush as well. I try not to think about the kind of conversation they might be having. Ezra probably won't be listening anyway. He loves The Woods — so many sticks and rocks.

I sit down in the newly vacated chair and rest my elbows on the island counter. "Anything I can do to help?" I ask. I know what my mother's response to this question will be, which is why I am willing to ask it. She never wants help. Any attempts at help are treated almost as insults, God bless her. If someone were to walk into my kitchen and ask me that question, I would hand them a list.

"No thanks, honey," she says. "What is Mitch up to today?"

I'm thinking a birdfeeder. Or maybe a birdhouse. One of those elaborate ones that look like a New England church or Victorian mansion. No, something more rustic. I have some soldering rods and rusty aluminum. I could make something manly out of metal with my propane blowtorch and some ingenuity. Okay, so it isn't the next great thing, but it's a start, a jumping off point. I have just fired up the blowtorch when I hear a pounding at the door. Fox doesn't wait for an answer, but just walks in. In his right hand he has a six pack of Miller High Life and in his left an oxy-acetylene torch. "I saw that the Subu was gone, man, so I thought you would be in here needing this," he says.

"The beer or the torch?" I say.

"Yeah, man. Exactly."

Fox's real name is Fergus (a family name handed down from father to son for generations) but the only person other than his mother to call him that got a split lip and a bloody nose before the "s" was out of his mouth. Even the teachers in school used to avoid the name by calling him Mr. MacPherson. In addition to the name Fergus, Fox also inherited from his Scottish ancestors a bright orange shock of hair, which was now thinning at the top but showing no signs of fading in color. We were best friends growing up — getting in fights on the playground in third grade, smoking doobies out my bedroom window in high school, always talking about girls neither of us would ever date — and even though we have next to nothing in common now, we know each other so well that it doesn't even matter.

"I'm not a certified welder, Fox. I don't know how to use that thing."

"What's to know? You turn this knob here, this knob here, light it with a flint striker, and you're off and running." Fox performs each of these actions as he's talking and then leans over with the lit torch to the nearest sheet of scrap metal and burns a smiley face into it. Then he smiles himself, turns off the torch, reaches into his back pocket and pulls out a baggie with two roaches in it. "I also brought a couple of these."

It is maybe three hours later, but I have lost all sense of time. The six pack is long gone and Fox and I sit comfortably amid a warm haze that only seeps out a little beneath the cracked garage door. The scrap metal has transmigrated from a birdhouse to a hulking, six-foot, abstract structure that Fox calls The Knight. It does somewhat resemble a suit of armor that has been thrown from a horse, trampled by a dragon, tossed into a burning volcano, and then left to sit out in the rain for twenty years.

Our discussion has transmigrated as well — from the definition of Art to more personal matters.

"Here's the thing," Fox is saying, "Do you know where my dad is right now? Right now, he's sitting on his smelly, old ass on his smelly, old recliner watching reruns of *Magnum, P.I.* and except for brief stints to the bathroom or the bedroom that is more or less where he's been since he retired five years ago. And I'm not going to say that he was a bad dad, but growing up, my brother and I saw him mostly on weekends and were made to feel like pests that he did his best to keep at arm's length. And I think he loves us, sure, and there were camping trips and fishing trips from time to time, but these were largely opportunities for him to point out our flaws and to yell at us. And where am I today? I'm an odd-job man who makes a little dough doing handy work for neighbors and acquaintances who don't want to shell out the kind of money it would take to hire a real professional. I live over my folks' garage, have two kids — different mothers — who I only see a few times a year, was married for about 16 seconds ten years back, and I think the only reason Steph agreed to marry me was because she thought I was dying of cancer. Shit, that's probably the only reason I married her, too. And those were the happiest six months of my life, when I thought that that brain tumor would finish me off. No pressure to be something I clearly wasn't going to be, no having to think of the future, everybody feeling sorry for me and shit. But then the fucking chemo actually worked despite all the odds being against it, and the joy that brought only lasted about two months, then, as they say, the party was over."

"Now, where are you at today? You went to college, got a good gig with the insurance company, got a smokn' hot wife who might be a bit of a hard ass, but at least she has a *hard ass*, two gorgeous kids, a nice house. I mean, there it is, man, the American fucking dream, and you're sitting out here in your garage with your loser pal from high school feeling bad about yourself and missing your daddy, who, if we're being honest here, was an asshole, and who you are probably much better off without, right? Right?"

A comfortable silence opens up between us: it's a silence of agreement, of harmony, of finally being able to see the world for how it is. I cough a little and squint at the heap of metal before us.

"It shouldn't be called The Knight," I say, "It should be called Father Figure."

Later, when asked about this moment, I will think that I recall a hissing, popping sound, but I can't be sure. I will remember nothing of the explosion, or of being blown fifty feet through the air to land in the Albrecht's front yard. I won't remember the gawking neighbors, or how the Keene's basset hound licks my forehead, or the arrival of the ambulances and fire trucks, and I will have been whisked away to the nearest hospital before the remains of Fox are zipped up in a body bag and taken to the morgue.

The onions Mom has started dicing for chili toppings are making my eyes sting, so I turn my head and look out the patio door and see Ezra and Larry making their way toward the house. It takes me a moment to understand what it is I am seeing. You know how sometimes when you wake up from a deep sleep and you think your alarm clock is a tornado siren or your spouse is a home invader and it takes a minute to get your bearings? It's kind of like that. My eyes are watery from the onions and the window is slightly fogged from the warmth of the kitchen, and I can see that Ezra is carrying something, but I can't tell what, and Larry is holding what I assume — what bloody well better just be — a BB gun, and I think, sonofabitch took my kid out to kill squirrels without asking my permission. But something is not reading right with the scene. Ezra is holding the "squirrel" oddly — reverently, with his hands outstretched before him — and Larry has a droopy, hangdog look about him, which is not a posture I have ever seen him wear. And then it hits me that it is not a squirrel that Ezra is carrying. It's Prissy.

When they enter the house, it is apparent to all that Prissy is dead. Among the list of childhood tragedies for which I have mentally prepared myself — broken bones, the loss or destruction of a favorite toy, a parental divorce, the realization that there is no Tooth Fairy, or Santa Clause, or God — the accidental slaughter by your own hand of your grandmother's cat is not among them, and I am at a loss for words. The silence that envelops the kitchen is thick enough to cut with the knife that Mom is still holding frozen in midair over a half-diced Vidalia. It is she who is the first to move, the first to break the silence, and even then, her words are mere whispers: *Oh, Prissy. Oh, dear. Oh, no. Oh, my. Goodness sake. Oh, my goodness sake. Oh, my heavens.* She moves on the wave of these whispers to advance toward Ezra and the cat, reaching out her hands to take his burden from him only to pull back at the last moment and clutch her hands to her chest. The tears standing in her eyes, I am certain, are not from the onion.

"Nana, I'm so sorry," Ezra finally says. We thought she was a squirrel. We saw the gray fur and the tail, and just thought she was a squirrel."

My Mom looks to Larry, but if she is hoping that he will add something, she is disappointed. He just looks at his muddy shoes and breathes loudly through his nose. By now, Audrey is standing in the doorway to the kitchen, the hush having been loud enough to draw her attention. "Holy, shit, Ez, you killed Hissy!" she says, and my mother is quick with an, "Audrey, language!" But now that the reality has been spoken we all breathe a little easier. There are words for our issue and now we just need to find a solution.

And then Ezra says, "I know you are sad right now, Nana, and might not be able to say yes or no yet, but I would like to be able to keep her. Have her mounted and keep her, I mean. I would take good care of her, and it would almost be like she was still alive."

Even Larry's eyes are dragged away from his shoes at this, and we all look at Ezra. Is this a different problem? Or is this a solution?

It has been almost a month since The Accident, and I think Nora is on the verge of forgiveness. It helps that the rubble of our former garage has been cleared away and the melted siding on the back of the house replaced. I don't know whether we will build a new garage or not, but if we do, it will be where we park the cars. I don't need a workshop anymore. It was the workshop that worked in me, not the other way around.

Fox. I wish I had been conscious after the explosion, that I could have held his hand and thanked him for all that he had done for me before he died, but from the accounts that I have read in the paper, it doesn't sound as if there would have been a hand to hold, or a life to thank. I was just barely able to make it to his funeral—heavily bandaged and medicated up to my eyeballs. I wanted to shake his dad's hand, but Nora thought that wasn't a good idea, for either his dad or my hand. Neither of Fox's parents seemed to pay me much attention, even though it had to have been obvious who I was from the bandages alone. Of course, I'm sure their minds were preoccupied with thoughts of their dear departed son; although his dad in particular seemed like he had someplace else he would rather be. Well, who wouldn't rather be someplace other than their own son's funeral?

Had Fox's dad been in Vietnam? I thought maybe he had. So maybe he understood me more on some level than most of the other people there could have. More so even than Nora, perhaps especially Nora, because as it turns out, Larry was right all along. Who would have guessed it?

Why did I get blown clear and Fox didn't? I admit that that is a thought that has kept me awake on more than one night since The Accident. I can only guess it means his work was done and mine isn't. And what is my work? I watch Ezra brush his teeth and climb into his pee-jays and know that that is where my work lies. It has been a crazy month for Ezra, what with shooting his grandmother's cat and having his father practically blow himself to kingdom come, but he seems to be taking it in stride. He likes the bandages that I still wear on my arms and to peek at the fresh pink skin that is growing underneath. The new Daddy, I tell him. They say that I will always have scars, but that's okay with me, and with Ezra, too. "Now, if anyone ever tries to pretend they are you and steal me away, I will always be able to know the real you from your scars," He says. "Nobody else would have scars like yours."

Some of The Knight/Father Figure survived the accident— lodged in the big, old oak tree in the side yard. It might kill the tree, but it might not. I think it looks great there, like it's emerging from the trunk to set out on its quest. Ezra calls it The Whacka-Boom.

"He's actually really good," I tell my mom. "He's upstairs right now putting Ezra to bed. Been a lot more hands-on with the kids—especially Ezra because Audrey's, you know, going through one of her J.D. Salinger phases. He seems at peace now, happy almost. It's amazing. We spent six thousand dollars on psychotherapy that made next to no difference and then his oldest friend blows himself up in our back yard and suddenly everything is coming up roses."

"Have you talked to him about it?"

"Of course I have. I mean, I've tried. He always says that it is something that I would have a hard time understanding, that his pre-Accident self wouldn't have been capable of understanding it. He says that only someone like Larry—of all people—would be able to understand, having been in Vietnam and everything."

"Larry wasn't in Vietnam."

"What are you talking about? Of course he was."

"No. Nope. His mother was a Canadian. Kept her citizenship. Larry had a dual citizenship. When it looked like we were going to get into Vietnam, she made him hoof it up to Ottawa with her. I never met Millicent, but from all accounts she wasn't a woman to brook arguments. Does he say that he was in Vietnam?"

"All the time, Mom! Are you kidding me?"

"Well, the whole affair is very embarrassing for him, poor thing. He's a vulnerable man. One of the reasons I fell in love with him. I hope you won't let on that I told you the truth. I would hate to think what it would do his self-esteem."

"*Larry's* self-esteem? Shit, Mom, what about Mitch? He thinks he's entered the hallowed halls of true manhood or something. He must think Ezra has, too, since he shot Prissy. Damnit, fucking Larry!"

"Language, Nora!"

"I have to go, Mom."

"Well, okay. I'll talk to you next week, then. Give the kids kisses for me."

Upstairs in his room, Ezra is getting settled in for the night. *Goodnight Moon* has been his favorite bedtime story since he was two, and even though he is five now, there are residual effects. It is his habit to say goodnight to all the objects in his room before going to sleep. "Goodnight, door. Goodnight, clock. Goodnight, books. Goodnight, rocks. Goodnight, Big Teddy. Goodnight, little teddy. Goodnight, bed. Goodnight, blanket. Goodnight, pillow. Goodnight, sippy cup. Goodnight, moon. Goodnight, stars." He reaches over and turns off his bedside lamp, "Goodnight, Prissy," and the base of the lamp—the eternally discontented Prissy—is cast into darkness.

A NAME I WILL NOT CALL MY DAUGHTER

When Granny Anne died
      her nightgown was ripped,
   stripped off
      her body sponged, cleaned of urine.
And after the funeral, the stories circled our house —
      Anne, who set the lace curtains on fire. Anne,
      shuttered behind doors,
Anne, who ran well on an electric shock. Anne,
      whose open arms I dashed away from.

      Now, when I witness my own fraying,
      I tongue your name, Anne. Forbidden sound.
      Imagine your secret place, under a breadfruit tree,
      Anne, your gold hoops
         clanging against your jaw.
      Anne, how you caress your broken things,
      that man who bruised
         then left you, his body
            dangling from the rafters.
      Anne, how you weep over your dreams,
      a house on a hill with a view
         of the sea, your children running
in the garden, flinging green mangoes at each other,
      their mouths full of your name,
         Mummy, Mummy, Mummy.

WHEN I FOLLOW GOD'S VOICE INTO THE DESERT

I hold onto one of my cheap gods.
Wooden with blue eyes, tied to my underwear,
I rub it against my crotch.

At the edge of the desert, near the highway,
Mary of Egypt preaches: *Eat locusts.*
Abstain from bread.

I watch cars speed by, spot a girl
with a big red lollipop. Her cheeks stained
with sweetness. How long
has it been since my tongue danced with sugar?

I count the silence of God, watch it thread, thicken
lengthen —

Mary of Egypt says, *God is never late.*
But she's whittled to hard bone and dust.

I came to hold God's thumb in my mouth,
the thickness and flesh of life.

At night, I dream of turning my idol
into a man. I eat him.
Lick clean his skin
until he is glowing red with my hunger.

71

RUSSIA THING

Investigations, notwithstanding

        your own unparalleled reporting,

have most of this town in a tizzy.

        You know how weak & fragile they all are,

afraid to speak or move

        unless they take a fall.

But what I really wanted to tell you

        before the next person comes along

& wants to go home

        is that liminality is often confused

with peering through the window at Andy's Deli

        & seeing a nest of warm piroshkis.

NEW MEDIA

No horn-rimmed lone intoner now. No grand
paterfamilias of evening news
shepherding watchers soberly toward views
moderate, monochrome, subdued, and bland.
Instead, kaleidoscopes! Mad movement crammed
down every microsecond. Wizards' brews
of weird conspiracy. Passions cut loose
in danse-macabre musics of the damned
that dun a ceaseless reverb in the skull,
hissing permission: *Feed the fire of your fear.*
Enrobe yourself in judgment, its long pall
swaddling you tight. Declare that you despise.
Lean on your narrow life as on a prayer.
Believe your barefaced heart, knowing it lies.

I said, "A goat? Are you sure
the cop didn't mean a boat?"

WHEN WE WERE SWASHBUCKLERS

"It is fitting that yesteryear's swashbuckling newspaper reporter has turned into today's solemn young sobersides nursing a glass of watered white wine after a day of toiling over computer databases in a smoke-free, noise-free newsroom."

— Russell Baker, former *New York Times* columnist

In the early '80s, on the phone with a congenial fire department spokeswoman I had come to know, I said, "Now I've got a personal question."

She took a deep breath, perhaps dreading I was going to invite myself over to her place for a glass of white Zinfandel, a jump in the Jacuzzi and a peacock feather backrub. "Shoot," she said.

I explained that I lived in an Anaheim apartment — without smoke detectors — with another reporter who enjoyed a beer and a cigarette or two in bed before he fell asleep. "What should I do if I wake up in my room and hear crackling flames and smell smoke?"

Keep as low as you can, she advised, and crawl quickly out the front door.

"What about my friend?"

"He's already a goner."

"You're sure?"

"Yup."

For a couple reasons, that wasn't the answer I wanted to hear. For one, Witty was a close buddy of mine. We were likened to Felix Unger and Oscar Madison in *The Odd Couple*. Secondly, if he was burned to cinder and bone, in the morning my editor — ever voracious for colorful tear-jerking copy—would compound my grief by ordering me to crank out twenty inches about the tragedy, most likely in minute-by-minute detail.

As a general assignment reporter, I had written plenty of first-person accounts: log-rolling on a lake against a champion dog at Knott's Berry Farm, waving a red cape in front of baby bulls in a Tijuana ring, immersing myself in Santa Ana's skid row with its missions and alleyways smelling of unwashed underpants. I was always a bumbling Everyman whose exploits were chronicled in self-deprecatory humor. But how would I describe myself if I kept low to the ground and slithered like a snake out the front door? If I wasn't a hero, would readers see me as a coward whose dereliction of duty should be derided in irate letters to the editor?

No, I'd have to make a heroic effort to save him. Stop in the bathroom, grab a ragged towel off the rack, soak it in brackish water dribbling from the rusting faucet and wrap it around my mouth, push open the door, crab walk into the inferno, and risk deadly inhalations by crying out his name. If he didn't answer, then I'd skedaddle . . . if I could. But what if I was engulfed in flames with the nearest extinguisher hanging outside on the earthquake-cracked wall near the mailboxes where my bills and rejection slips were delivered? Then someone else—maybe even one of my rivals—would get the front-page byline.

And what would the gossips say about Dave Witty and me dying in the same bedroom? While I'm not homophobic, I wouldn't want malicious reporters—and there were many of them in the newsroom—suggesting my image as a ladies' man was all a facade.

Witty being Witty, he might cross up my heroic efforts by rescuing himself: shattering his bedroom window with his well-thumbed dictionary, springing through the sharded opening and leaping into the over-chlorinated swimming pool, invigorated by the excitement. Suddenly I would be the fool who—by shoving open the door—fed new oxygen to the fire, intensifying an inferno that would char me to a crisp.

What kind of story would Witty be expected to write? One with lots of facts. I was the reporter assigned to profile the Fullerton truck driver who swerved his truck off an icy Midwestern road to keep from crushing a family sedan that had wandered across a slick grassy median and lost a leg when his cab flipped over. Witty was a hard-news reporter who relished zoning feuds, petty ideological spats and bank robberies attempted by hungry old men armed with cap pistols. He'd mention a few of my journalistic achievements, list the costs of the destruction, cite county-wide statistics about fire fatalities, and at length quote firefighters pontificating about the harm wreaked by backdrafts and the stupidity of someone dashing into flames in a t-shirt, cutoff jeans and flip-flops, even with a wet towel over his mouth. As Witty wrote this story, he'd take regular breaks to smoke a cigarette.

In newspaper jargon, a rumpled, hard-driven reporter has ink coursing through his veins. If so, the first dark droplets entered my bloodstream when I was ten years old. Reigning like a benevolent prince when visiting Southern California, my uncle, Robert Day, generously doled out five-dollar bills at a time when my three sisters and I made do with dime allowances. But money wasn't what I hungered for. He was a *New Yorker* cartoonist and I wanted him to bless the caricatures I spread around Grandma Day's house. He preferred to maintain his silence, not wanting to wound me or give me false hope.

At Uncle Robert's departure, I knew I could no longer say I wanted to be a cartoonist when I grew up. To brighten my mood, Mom said, "Why don't you become a journalist?" My blue eyes widened at the majesty of that word, and my destiny was writ in ink. Ballpoint ink scrawled across narrow notepads. Typewriters in need of fresh ribbons. Presses rolling out my words and bylines.

Over the next decade, I produced a thousand column inches for a church newsletter, the Latin Club *Acta Diurna*, and the school papers at my junior high, senior high, and college. Not without controversy (for I wanted to rouse readers instead of boring them), I edited the Glendale High *Explosion* and Cal State L.A.'s *College Times* (which was probably the first university paper to publish the word "screw" in a sexual sense).

In college, my assistant Baxter and I assigned our reporters stories about the various aspects of thievery on campus. Proving the lack of bookstore security, a short, innocent-looking blonde wrote a first-person account about the ease of tucking a globe under her coat and waddling past the smiling checkout clerk, looking like she was months overdue.

In high school I decided that though I relished the instant gratification of writing for newspapers, I possessed a higher calling: literary fiction in the tradition of ex-newsmen like Ernest Hemingway, Charles Dickens and George Orwell. Hunching over a Remington portable, inspired by the lyricism and schoolboy depictions of William Golding's *Lord of the Flies*, I began a novel about junior high, *Too Old, Too Young*.

Before my final year of state college, I banked enough money — earned laboring the previous two summers for the railroad that employed Dad as a clerk — to focus on my literary words. At a time when Witty was still in elementary school, I finished my novel hours before boarding the first of the trains that would carry me — without the luxury of a Pullman berth — from Los Angeles to New York City with the manuscript of my novel on my lap and a sack of bologna sandwiches and a large can of Hawaiian Punch at my feet.

On Long Island, I stayed with Uncle Robert and Aunt Ethel in their stately home. On the day my uncle drove his blue Mercedes into the city to deliver a stack of drawings to *The New Yorker*, I presented my novel to the secretary of a leading publishing house. I wanted to be a famous serious writer by the time I graduated in the spring of '67, and then type masterpieces in a rough-hewn cabin on an island mountaintop not far from a beach where I could body surf and recite poetry to a tanned, ethereal Muse. During the Great Depression, my uncle moved across the country with only a portfolio of his work, and now his drawings shared pages with the words of J.D. Salinger, Muriel Sparks and John Updike. So why couldn't my dream come true, too?

The next decade I was whipsawed by setback after setback. I wrote a half-dozen unpublished novels. Though I was sentenced to probation instead of prison by a sympathetic judge, I was convicted of a felony because I refused to be drafted into the Army to fight in a senseless war. The right-wing *San Gabriel Valley Tribune*—mere blocks from my home— wouldn't even give me a perfunctory job interview, no doubt aware of the controversies I stirred in college.

After graduation, I worked as a YMCA camp director, folk singer, and rec leader for handicapped kids. Seeking experiences to weave into my novels and stricken with wanderlust, I quit these jobs to thumb around North America and hop freight trains to New Orleans. Hitchhiking, I developed my interviewing and storytelling abilities. If I made a driver laugh or kept him talking, he might buy me a burger and take me beyond his original destination.

When I was burdened by onerous attorney fees and feeling only the sale of my latest novel could save me, Dad again used his influence to find me a job for which I was totally inept: railroad carpenter. Living frugally with my parents and selling the motorboat I won on *Let's Make a Deal* dressed as a frog, I climbed out of debt and financed a year-long backpacking trip around the world. Back home, I bought a used VW Super Beetle, and looked for my first newspaper job and apartment at age twenty-eight.

By '74, the Vietnam War had become unpopular enough that my conviction didn't seem to matter to the *Whittier Daily News* editors. In a newsroom of burned out reporters perpetually grumbling about our low wages and their need for a second job, I was an energetic producer of copy and photography. One afternoon Chuck the city editor asked my fellow reporters to lower their grumbling because they were disturbing me while I typed like Clark Kent on crystal meth.

Somedays I literally typed for eight hours with a quick break for lunch . . . and then went to my part-time job as rec leader at an institution housing mentally ill and disabled adults. One elderly woman — who looked like my kindly Aunt Frona — occasionally got the urge to grab men between their legs. She sat beside my friend Rich when he gave a slide presentation of his travels. In the dark, I could hear Rich titter and slap her wandering hand. I had to bite my lip to keep from howling with laughter.

I wrote every story imaginable to fill the *Daily News'* maw: the collision of two airplanes above a schoolyard, a description of the swimsuits worn by young women that summer at the Whittier College pool, the opening day of Little League, a page-filling article about game show contestants, including my own disillusioning experience trying to claim my motorboat.

Mornings the reporter with the cop beat phoned me to read newsworthy items from the logbook, and then I'd shape the information into stories. One day he described an accident involving "a truck hauling a goat." I said, "A goat? Are you sure the cop didn't mean a boat?" "Nope, it's definitely a goat." "You sure?" "That's a 'g' for goat." I sighed, yielding to his authority, and wrote the brief. The next day he returned from the station and told me, "You were right. It was a boat."

In a newsroom without windows (lest we daydream), I wrote weather stories that had zero chance of giving our readers an accurate forecast. Relying on information from a news service, I made predictions that would've seemed laughable if only I bothered to poke my head outside. Sometimes I prophesized evening rainfall when the sky was cloudless and the wind was dead. For local temperatures, I was told to report the often disparate readings from a nearby bank and the thermometer on our sun-reflecting roof. On a day our metal roof could've fried eggs, I wrote that the country's hottest temperatures were experienced by Whittier and Death Valley.

Known as Richard Nixon's hometown, Whittier was a notoriously conservative community founded by Quakers. So when a flamboyant funeral was planned for a member of the Scavengers motorcycle gang, Chuck assigned me to cover it with the hopes he could sneak my story past Mel, the gruff managing editor.

Buzzed by the beer Grease's cohorts insisted I guzzle in their club house, I wrote a piece describing Grease's sedate Catholic Mass, the parade of Heathens, Vulcans, and Hell's Angels to the cemetery, and the raucous burial of his Harley, casket and offerings that included beer cans, a gun, and joints of marijuana.

Our scheme to publish the story was dependent on a female reporter working alongside Mel on the copy desk on Saturday, when neither Chuck nor I were on duty. Chuck told her not to show my article to Mel, and I gave her my phone number and insisted she call if she had the slightest question. So what happened? She had a question, and passed the story to Mel, who read it, harrumphed and spiked it. Monday Mel praised the story, but said it didn't fit with Whittier's image of itself. An angry Scavenger phoned to ask me why my tribute to Grease hadn't run. I explained the situation and the Scavenger wondered out loud if he and some of his buddies should teach this Mel a lesson. "No, no," I said. "That would only get *me* in trouble."

I received a press pass for an event I knew I couldn't write about: the Miss Nude USA beauty pageant. At the Treehouse Fun Ranch in the desert, I learned female nudity can be boring and male nudity can be repulsive. One of the day's highlights was the descent of a group of nude male skydivers, whose primary objective was to avoid landing on a cactus.

A year's toil in Whittier earned me a spot at the *Santa Monica*

Evening Outlook, where I profiled the bandleader Lawrence Welk, who played his accordion for me. I also wrote about Spud, a homeless guy who slept beside a liquor store in his wheelchair, and covered the rescue of a harbor patrolman who went missing aboard a 14-foot skiff one night after its motor malfunctioned and winds pushed him out to sea.

One day I was given an assignment that would antagonize the managing editor, Ron, who was known for impetuously firing reporters. My investigation exposed the prejudice of the hoity-toity Jonathan Club, whose powerful white non-Jewish men often made deals at classy locations in Los Angeles and Santa Monica. The Air Force Academy's Catholic Cadet Choir was invited to enjoy an afternoon at the beach club until a black cadet was discovered in its ranks. When Ron tried to soften my articles, I vainly resisted the changes, beginning a downward slide toward termination.

My fledgling newspaper career seemed over. I spent weeks putting together jigsaw puzzles until I was hired to work for a public relations firm in Marina del Rey. While living a lavish lifestyle by mixing his funds with the company's, the owner bounced checks to vendors. To celebrate George Washington's birthday at Washington Fashion Square, I decided to create the largest cherry pie west of the Mississippi. A fancy bakery donated the crust, only asking we reimburse them for the cost of the immense tin. Meanwhile my boss billed the center for the cost of the entire event, and spent much of the money elsewhere, possibly on his East African safari. After the celebration, the baker repeatedly talked to our secretary without satisfaction. By mistake I once answered the baker's call. I could only stammer, "Pie tin? I don't know anything about a pie tin."

When vendors started calling me direct, I quit.

No doubt disturbed by my implosion, my live-in girlfriend finished her teaching credential and got a job and her own apartment in the desert. I moved into a condo in Santa Ana with one of my sisters. I was given a lead on a job wholesaling products for Johnson & Johnson, but first I tried the local papers. *The Register* kept me from peddling baby powder and panty shields.

Soon enough, over foamy pitchers of Budweiser at O'Hara's pub, I informally joined a band of male and female swashbucklers. From the Santa Ana Mountains to the sands of Seal Beach, we swaggered across Orange County, armed with leaky pens instead of the cutlass swung by Errol Flynn in *Captain Blood*. Our printed words were meant to protect the poor, glorify heroes, bring down villains dressed in fancy suits, expose governmental waste, and unmask clergymen who worshipped Mammon. If drunken brigands were about to ravish a damsel, we would've fought her free with pica sticks and smoldering cigarettes, and then written about it for the evening edition.

For a first-person series about the down-and-out denizens of Santa Ana's skid row, I spent several days sleeping in a fetid mission dorm, earning a few dollars by taking day labor jobs, shaving in the library, and subjecting myself to "ear-bangings" from preachers who pictured the hellfire that waited sinners like ourselves.

As part of my series, I included a Beggars-Can-Be-Choosy Guide to free dining spots. The maximum of four coffee cups (heaven sent) was awarded the Peniel Mission for its tasty bean soup, savory fish patty, finger-singeing potatoes, and choice of ice cream, though "preceding the meal was a Bible-belting sermon capable of knotting your stomach and killing your appetite." One cup (desperation time) was given the Rescue Mission for its breakfast of dry, cold doughnuts, and dinners that were a chore to chew.

My series won awards, but not everyone praised it. A reader named Louis wrote in part, "Your frivolous little hike with the hobos was more depressing to us than to yourself. Depressing in the sense, that as a staff writer, you so unwittingly provoked your readers with the unnecessary revelation that your faith in God, if indeed you possess any at all, is shallow as Hen Piss. You should have been beaten unmercifully for invading the habitation of derelicts, unrighteously utilizing their source of food, bedding ..."

My series led to a family reunion for a gray-bearded ex-con named Art, who was quoted as saying he could get his life together if only he had a roof over his head, three square meals a day, and a job. From a photo of him eating chicken beside the railroad station, Art was recognized by a brother. After the series ran, Art hunted me down at the paper to ask for a handout. I told him I had a surprise for him instead . . . and drove him to his brother's house. Grown used to nestling in the grass, that night he had trouble sleeping in a bed. Art had assumed his mom was dead and he'd never see her again, but she re-entered his life, too. Within months, though, he shed his new life—with its leisure suits, sit-down dinners and familial expectations—and returned to the streets. The family celebrated Christmas without him. I'm not sure if his mom ended her prayer as she had before her son was found: "And God, please bless the one who isn't here."

After he joined our swashbuckling band at *The Reg* in '78, Witty and I bonded on the newsroom softball team. He was a bandy-legged slap hitter who wore his "Half-Witty" nickname on his jersey when we played other papers, various companies and even county jail inmates. An advantage of being incarcerated was always having a home field advantage: a short right field fence that beckoned a lineup packed with left-handed batters, plus a vociferous crowd and the reward of a Coke if they won. As catcher, I once caught a long throw as an inmate sped toward home plate, and planted my cleats in the dirt. He wound up his arm and unsuccessfully tried to punch the ball out of my glove. At least a vision of a Coke hadn't turned his fist upward into my nose. A fight could've caused a riot in which our pampered typing fingers would have battled dozens of pointed shanks and bladed shivs.

On the field and in the newsroom, Witty was an intense cheerleader. He was thin, an inch or so shorter than my five-foot-ten-and-a-half, with greasy black hair, oily skin dotted with a few acne scars, and rotten teeth he boasted he never brushed. His voice often had a strange gurgling sound as if he was speaking underwater. After cutting himself shaving, many days he showed up in the newsroom with specks of blood on his white shirt collar. He looked every bit the unkempt reporter I remembered from black-and-white movies I watched on TV as a kid: *Front Page, Scandal Sheet,* and *Deadline – USA*."

Once Witty told me, "I suppose I became a reporter because it was the only thing I was good at." Without the draft to worry about, he rose swiftly from the college paper to a small daily to *The Reg,* where he first covered several school districts and then was assigned a major city beat.

Reporting on a school board meeting, Witty described an altercation in which one member punched another one. Alas, he got them backward, telling half a million that the man who got clocked had taken the swing. Witty was relieved when he wasn't sued. As one ex-colleague recalled, "Witty loved facts, but he didn't always stick to them."

There were lots of remarkable personalities in that dreary, cavernous newsroom. If Witty represented extroversion, crime reporter J.J. Mahoney — who would eventually be felled by the effects of chain smoking — embodied introversion. He likely learned to keep to himself during three years in reform school and thirteen years in prison. While incarcerated for a murder and armed robbery he committed at nineteen, he became an artist, poet and *Kansas City Star* book reviewer. A day after he was paroled, J.J. became a reporter for the *Star*. At *The Reg,* he was renowned for his stories about two "freeway killers," William Bonin (who tortured, raped and murdered at least twenty-one boys and young men, and was executed in 1996) and Randy Craft (who lives in San Quentin's death row for slaying at least sixteen young men).

Reading about Bonin's predilection for picking up male hitchhikers, sodomizing and then stabbing them to death, I thought of my "Orman on the Road" series, in which I crisscrossed Orange County by thumbing, walking, and riding local buses, interviewing people along the way: a young couple vacationing at a nudist camp off Ortega Highway, an elderly woman who lived on buses, and an artist whose philosophy was formed when he was fourteen and his dad showed him how to become a hobo riding the rails. For transportation and housing during those three weeks, I depended on the kindness of strangers. Luckily, one of them wasn't a freeway killer.

In competition with the Orange County edition of the *Los Angeles Times*, the owners of *The Reg* decided to make major changes. New editors were brought in. Typewriters, gluepots, scissors and copy paper were replaced with computers. Pages were redesigned and color was added. Salaries were raised. Old-timers in the photo department were replaced with a young team that would win a Pulitzer a few years later for its coverage of the '84 Olympics in Los Angeles. The owners' libertarian politics were even confined to the opinion pages. Plans were made for a new building with cubicles for reporters instead of rows of desks without partitions.

Naturally new editors wanted to prove their importance by bringing in reporters they had overseen at other publications and giving them plum assignments that previously had gone to the likes of myself. Some of my swashbuckling friends didn't survive these changes. One photographer was last seen driving a taxi at John Wayne Airport.

Thinking with my heart instead of my head, I moved into an Anaheim condo with my girlfriend Lindy—an astrologer who was a Leo—and her three kids. A year later, I still couldn't bring myself to give up what was left of my travel goals and commit to marriage. She evicted me just as Witty's roommate was moving out of his apartment.

Just like that . . . Witty and I became the Odd Couple, except that neither of us was a neat-freak. I was messy and he was messier, the difference being that he scattered his empty beer cans and cigarette butts and ash everywhere. Astrologically we were both fixed signs, but he was a passionate, spittle-spraying, sarcastic Scorpio (think Leon Trotsky and Charles Manson) and I was a cool Aquarian (think Jack Lemmon and Paul Newman).

As he smoked his first cigarette of the day at the kitchen table, he liked nothing more than to dissect even the most insignificant story in the day's paper, which he had already devoured. After work, if I told him I wanted to lose a couple pounds, he'd fry up some steaks and spoon me a heaping bowl of cookies 'n cream. While sipping beer and sharing a joint, he questioned me about the women I was wooing. He never mentioned a love interest of his own, though his voice caught whenever he mentioned the name of a reporter he once dated. If I yawned and excused myself to go to my room, he'd reel me back by asking if I wanted to hear about a clandestine romance between two unlikely reporters.

At least eight marriages sprang from the newsroom. Not all of them were successful. Donna and Gary's wedlock was quickly and acrimoniously sundered, but they had to continue working with each other. Their solution? A reporter named Barry sat between them as their conduit relaying messages back and forth. They're both now in that Great Newsroom in the Sky, where I hope they're on speaking terms.

Whenever I could, I urged Witty to quit his job and travel the world, accumulating experiences that would make him a better journalist. He shook his head and said he'd always worked since he was a kid growing up in Davis. But he loved to hear my travel tales: being thrown in the squalid New Orleans jail with my folk-singing partner Rich during Mardi Gras, interviewing the Dalai Lama when I hauled my backpack into the Himalayas to escape

India's fierce heat, stuffing newspapers into my clothes to keep warm in a boxcar.

One day Witty was crestfallen. His journalistic hero and former professor, Gary Granville was being shoved out of his metro editor position into a sedate position because workaholic tendencies were ruining his health. Without expecting him to agree, I suggested Witty become a vagabond. Much to my surprise, he immediately organized a garage sale, and swore he was going to visit more countries than me. Perhaps his emphatic decision was Fate's way of snuffing out a three-alarm fire before it could begin.

I explained my plight to a pretty teller at my bank. After twisting her lips to the side, she said she and a girlfriend rented a house in Garden Grove, and their roommate just moved out. She said they didn't want someone with furniture other than a bed and dresser. My face lit up. Instantly I moved from *The Odd Couple* to *Three's Company*, the sitcom about a single man living with two single women.

Witty meandered across America until he settled in New York City. Every possible hour he entered data for a law firm. His corroded teeth were filed and filled inexpensively by students at a school of dentistry. (Proving years later that you get what you pay for, while teaching English in Taiwan he sneezed and a temporary tooth flew across the classroom and bounced against a student's face.)

Pinching his pennies and nickels, Witty lived in cramped squalor in a huge, decrepit apartment building. Our mutual friend David Ferrell visited him for a week in the early '80s. Walking down the hallway to Witty's room, Ferrell held his breath to keep from inhaling an unbearable stench likely given off by a dead creature in the wall.

When Witty turned on his clock radio, a rock song blared from the front and cockroaches scurried out the back. As they tumbled out of their living quarters, Witty said matter-of-factly,

"They don't like the music."

The horrors continued when the two Davids went out for pizza. During the meal, Ferrell felt something on the back of his neck and swatted at it. A cockroach—probably one of Witty's roommates—fell into his shirt, forcing him frantically to yank out his shirttail. Wisely Ferrell slept at the Waldorf Astoria, where his bill was comped by the hotel because he was writing a travel story for the paper.

Freed of hacking out objective, straight-forward news accounts about school boards and city council, Witty let his creativity soar when he wrote letters. On the back of an envelope, he scribbled, "Written while intoxicated with life, booze, ecstasy, good music, and all that sort of stuff."

Reversing our roles, he wrote, "You burnout shell of an old man. You *Register* lifer, shuck off your chains of despair and suffering. Quit the paper. Buy a new backpack. Feast your eyes on my map."

Witty didn't know my eyes were already feasting on a map. In less than two years, I quit *The Reg*, and headed by land to the tip of South America on a difficult journey—largely by rickety bus—of eleven months. When I returned, I still had money in the bank because dealing on the black market with my dollars had made the trip inexpensive. So I took off for a six-week sojourn in China and Tibet.

With his savings, Witty traveled through Europe, Africa and Asia, often on a bike. Two years after I traveled in China and Tibet, he hitched there with a Dutch woman who returned to Holland with a baby in her womb. When he was teaching English in Taiwan, we resumed our correspondence by e-mail.

Of one excursion, he wrote in 2002, "I jumped on ye olde motorcycle and rode across the island. It's a grueling seven-hour ride, almost all through the mountains. I was up so high at one point there was snow on the ground and my hands were frozen even though I was wearing ski gloves. What makes it even more grueling is that I cross the island in one day, spend the night in a hotel, and come back the next. Of course I ease the rigor by taking a fistful of joints with me and there's always a sack of beer on ice dangling from my handlebars."

Still, Witty admitted he had become a creature of comfort. "I'm soft and I like to pamper myself. I've had more than my share of riding on the tops of trains or in the backs of trucks crammed like a sardine in a can."

In September of 2011, in a three-way conversation with Ferrell, I e-mailed them a quote from President Lyndon Johnson, "The fact that a man is a newspaper reporter is evidence of some flaw of character."

I asked what flaws we might've possessed. "Generally speaking," answered Ferrell, "as newspaper reporters, we were too loud, too egotistical, too disorganized, too frantic and we drank and partied too much." Witty said he fit that portrayal to a T.

And then my messages went unanswered. Two months later, I gasped when I opened an e-mail from his friend Joshua, "On November 3, 2011, a few days after his 56th birthday. Cause of death was sarcoma. Cremation ceremony, with a few of David's Taichung friends, in the hills."

Roy from the Glendale High *Explosion*. Baxter from the *College Times*. Nick and Witty from *The Register*. All of them close friends. All of them swashbucklers with newsprint on their fingers and elbows. All of them gone too soon. If they were still here, I'd make them laugh by describing my interview with a talking cat.

ELEVATION

The near-mile between our bodies
and sea level was a fact with consequences

I could not understand: my loaves burned
at the edges and oozed from the center, offensive

as yolk upon the blade of a whetted knife.
Each week, I stopped at the downtown bakery

to spirit flour-speckled rye, pumpernickel, brioche
into crisp, white paper, into warm and costly bundles;

what astonishing weight, broken by your hands
at supper with a creak like bones after no sleep,

fingertips shoveling in toward
your wobbling, unleavened breast.

TEXACO OPERA

At Grandpa's Texaco Station, I loved Saturday night's sound:
the ding of gas pump bell and a pure soprano voice
blurred memory of kerosene smell and pipe smoke.
Notes whispering from his big radio like chills or snippet of dream
my face like grandpa's, in faraway reverie, lips lifting,
smiling at new rooms opening in our head, rising from the notes.

It was the women who drew me, heart tethered to their notes,
male voices leaving me unmoved, impatient with their dark sound
discovering then the escape offered by treble lines lifting,
eyes closed, high above black lace sky, shyly testing my voice.
The Metropolitan Opera was unreal as wealth, a dream
where women in lavish dresses made music visible as smoke.

Grandpa was a long way from coal-camp smoke —
even further from polished pages of his calligraphy left in love notes,
long way from gorgeous European cities of his soldier day
    dreams —
coal trucks on 23, Clinchfield train whistle blasting background
    sound —
shrill earsplitting noise, nothing like magic Renee Fleming's
    unearthly voice
drowning it all out every Saturday night by fireside with pipe
    smoke lifting.

Maria Callas and Joan Sutherland, even their names brought a
    lifting.
Carmen, Figaro, Madame Butterfly, Don Giovanni fill my head like
    smoke.
They sang in foreign tongue, yet I still recognized the voice.
Writing letters only to burn them in *La Boheme*, Tosca dies while
    writing notes.
Even so young, I see in words and tunes the power of sound,
the way hand, lips, tongue and heart could create a daylight dream.

To return here to his boyhood home had been Grandpa's
    fevered dream
only his father's death made possible long night's lifting.
Like Tosca he found hope for a future in the turning key sound
of his father's farmhouse door, a remembered fireplace
    spreading hope in the smoke.
Heart overflowing, writing all his soldier friends excited notes,
he told how he'd escaped the drudgery of coal, found a
    businessman's voice.

Sitting by the stove, I remember the woman at church with her
    noon bell voice.
To sing of poets, geisha girls, soldiers and fair maids, a
    wondrous dream.
It would take a lot of growing to hold those notes,
my own little prayed secret, one nobody would be lifting.
In coal camp, nothing's pretty and chimneys spew black gritty
    smoke.
I needed to be near music, not trains or coal trucks' sound.

A little blonde girl huddles a kerosene stove, notes lifting
the voice in her head straight to heaven with grandpa's pipe smoke
treble trill and stunning vibrato fueling dreams of living inside that sound.

HOW TO REINCARNATE

first, start by taking back
all the birthday wishes you ever gave
ever

then, unwind
the grunt and *good morning* head-nods,
the *I respect you* handshakes

rip off the sympathetic bandages
and hold up a raw palm to strangers,
refusing to hear them out

you have been too kind
and too willing to move aside for them,
like a flimsy bead curtain

so re-invent yourself in this bar,
where the music melts away by drips
like ice-cubes in a tumbler

avoid yourself in the tilted mirror,
you are older than you have never been
and so tired

flirt only with a fresh beard,
ignore the broken pocket comb
and the rasp of after-hours stubble

and all the while, whisper to yourself
I am home now, this is where I belong

*"Barbie here says we can take this handsome
young fellow for a walk."*

ANTIMATTER

My daughter Nora is studying antimatter. I think about this, usually in the evening, on the nights when Ben works late and I feel uncertain. Nora calls me once a week from school and she tells me about her classes. When I ask, she explains antimatter is material that, if brought into contact with ordinary matter, destroys it in an unhappy burst of radiation. "Antimatter," Nora says, "acts like ordinary matter. *Except . . .*"

"Except what?" I say. "Does it know that it's different?"

Sometimes I wonder what Jilly would make of this, and by this I mean everything. Jilly was the first friend I made after my husband Ben and I moved here, and for awhile I thought that maybe, besides Ben, she was the person who knew me best.

Back then, I was a new mother, and lonely; to say I missed Milwaukee is an understatement. I met Jilly Ginter at one of Ephrem's Park District Mommy & Me classes. It was an excellent play group by Ephrem standards, a place where children learned and grew, right on schedule, as any of the best mothers would attest. There was a singing circle and a dress-up corner. There was "free play," my least favorite time, because while the other mothers chatted and laughed about parenting (these women were so *confident*), I kept on playing one-on-one with my girl. Sometimes the play group teacher, a no-nonsense mom of teen boys, as I learned, would come and sit with the two of us while we pushed trains across the rug. But her kindness felt like pity, and she had to mingle with the other mothers, too. It's not that they weren't polite, these other women; they were born polite. But I am, as Ben has said (with love), always myself. These "nice moms" made such a meal of the class, and I didn't seem to understand the rules.

On the day I met Jilly, I was standing outside the classroom after we were done. A tiny brunette whose son appeared in local ads for a toy train was surreptitiously giving directions to a get-together at her house, which was walking distance from the Park District building and thus desirable: it was in the "older" section of town, which meant, essentially, that the houses hadn't all been built from the same plan. It had been clear since day one that she was the sun in this mom universe; the other mothers circled her like dwarf planets and copied the way she dressed, which was usually yoga pants and some sort of zip-up. The trick, apparently, was to not look like you tried too hard. On the surface of things, Toy Train's mother was casualness itself. She was also tiny and looked hot in those pants. What she said, went.

Not everyone was invited to her house, for instance, to eat chicken salad diced so fine it was fluffy (I heard). I imagined organic juice for the kids, maybe even cocktails for the moms. (The cocktails, they were a thing, even in Ephrem. Especially in Ephrem.) On this day, when she took pains to draw the other women aside to extend her invitation, I told myself it wasn't personal, and that she was probably only inviting the boys her son played with in class. Then I watched her whisper to the mom of a little girl named Ava. Ava was an ill-tempered child with a starved look to her; Nora was so much sweeter! I looked at my nails, which had dirt under them. I'm sweet too, is what I thought.

"Fuck her," someone said in my ear, and when I turned there was Jilly. I'd seen her in class and been struck by her demeanor, which was that of not giving a shit. Now here she was: tall and heavy, wearing baggy gray sweatpants and a tight-fitting man's overcoat. An astrakhan hat was jammed over her curls. "The McDonald's at the Ephrem Mall has a great Play Place," she said. "Want to take the kids?"

I thought about what I usually did after class, which was get Nora home and make us both peanut butter sandwiches, then maybe visit a park. The other mothers kept their kids busy: there were swim classes and karate and soccer camp; one kid was learning Chinese. But I played with Nora at the park, usually miles from the subdivision where we lived, to reduce the chances of our running into people we barely knew. I wanted friends — I did! — but there were a lot of ways to bungle it with these mothers, who wielded uncanny power.

Besides, if I was different, Nora was more so. She was so smart she saw the world in a breathtakingly different way, but this wasn't something I had figured out yet. Not then. What I saw was that other children didn't seem to understand her or the abstract way she looked at things. The puns she loved bewildered them, for example, and I was vigilant during play dates, in case I was called upon to protect her. Sometimes it was just easier to be alone, us two. Sometimes we'd drive 45 minutes to find a park where we could be anonymous: in one of the small towns west of Ephrem, or another subdivision, maybe, and in my memory the sun is always out and we are usually alone. We'd swing on the swings and play pretend — just the two of us. Nora was four, and I was in my forties. I knew there wouldn't be another.

But that day, I looked at the nicotine stains on Jilly's fingers, the net of ancient acne scars on her cheeks, and I said, "Sounds fun." Jilly always kept to herself in the class, but the way she did it made it seem like a choice. "I'm Michelle." I stuck out my hand. "My friends call me Micky," I added.

We went to McDonald's and ordered Happy Meals for the kids. The orange plastic chairs were kid-sized, bolted to the floor, and if it was a relief that Jilly joked about squeezing into "these fucktaqua chairs" even as she super-sized her fries, it was better still that we went on to talk about something besides parenting. Jilly, it turned out, was a voracious reader. We both liked horror novels and we both liked movies and we both liked to think there was more to us than motherhood.

When I asked her if she felt bad that we'd been excluded

from Toy Train's play date, she just stared. "You're telling me you *want* to be there, Micky?" After that, I knew that Nora and I always would have someone to hang out with after class. I am private by nature but with Jilly I threw myself headlong into candid, speculative gossip, usually about Toy Train's mother and her supplicants.

What did we say? Oh, it was harmless stuff, for the most part. "Botox face," I might whisper to Jilly about another mother's smooth brow, and Jilly would snort with laughter. We joked about our own homes, which weren't downtown like Toy Train's house; we pretended devastation that the trees in our neighborhood weren't as big, or as nice, as the ones on Toy Train's street. "Well our trees came from Mother Nature's asshole, of course," Jilly would deadpan. She was funny! She was brave.

The four of us usually went to McDonald's, where needless to say we never saw the other moms. I had my own reservations about the "chicken" nuggets and plastic toys, but it was a relief to have a friend to talk to. And Jilly's Kyle was kind to my Nora, who in Kyle's company ran and skipped and pretended to be a pony named Daisy. I told Jilly about my mom, who had survived two recurrences of cancer only to learn there might now be spots on her lungs. Jilly, being Jilly, bought me a milkshake and announced that cancer could go fuck itself.

She was cheerful when she said it, which was, it turned out, exactly what I needed. She was cheerful in general, but one day, one of the first really warm days when I let Nora leave her sweater at home, Jilly was quiet all through the Park District play group. No jokes about Botox. No laughing, period. After class let out, when I suggested we go get "the usual," she hesitated for a split second before shrugging, yes.

But she wasn't herself. Not when we ordered our burgers, not when we found our usual seats near the Play Place slides. I asked Jilly what she was reading but she sighed and picked at her fries. Finally the kids ate what they were going to and ran off to climb through the maze of tubes.

With the kids gone, our table was quiet. I looked through the cloudy plate-glass window, which faced south towards the fields. We'd buy corn here in August, I thought. At one of those stands. I thought about how the other moms had been laughing about something at class, a shared joke, something from the previous weekend. So when Jilly said, "Doug's talking about getting a dog," I was only half listening.

Doug was Jilly's husband. He was a cop, with a dead tooth right up front that made his smile seem strange.

"A dog," I said. I don't like dogs, and talking about them bored me.

"He's on about that murder," Jilly said. "You know." My ears pricked up then. A local teacher had been killed around Easter, and Jilly's husband was involved with the case.

"He is *so* stressed," Jilly said. "He says a dog would calm him down. Maybe it would. He had a dog when he was a kid." She ran her fingers through her hair, which was dense and wiry and threaded with gray; it rose from her head in a bristling column, like something alive.

Doug had been one of the officers who'd come on the scene when the teacher's husband called. I remembered that now.

I looked at Jilly and thought about an ad I'd seen on television the other day. In the ad, there was a woman who looked like Toy Train's mother. She was holding a platter of pancakes, which she set down on the kitchen table, in front of a man in a polo shirt and two children, a boy and a girl. Everyone was smiling hysterically.

"I thought I'd go look at dogs," Jilly said. "You know, scope out the shelter."

"Every boy needs a dog," I said. I thought about how in the commercial, the pancakes all rolled off the plate. Even though the sound on the television was turned low, I could tell the pancakes were singing: they had little faces made of butter and syrup. The family was clapping. There was a pitcher of orange juice, too, rocking rhythmically back and forth.

I'd given Nora soda with breakfast the other day. We were out of juice and I told myself soda couldn't be any worse than some of the sugared cereal out there. I thought about how messy my house was, and how Jilly didn't care about that. The Play Place was bright and I shaded my eyes with my hand; there Nora and Kyle were, wedged onto a platform and whispering to one another.

"I'll go look at dogs with you," I said.

We went to Ephrem's animal shelter, which was located not far from where the play group met, and a husky woman in an orange smock looked us up and down before leading us to the back where the dogs were. Jilly ignored the puppies, which everyone likes, and focused in on a muscular dog with a ruined ear. He was a real sweetheart, the woman in the smock told us.

"I like the underdogs," Jilly said, eyeing the torn ear.

"I know you do," I said, then looked over at Nora and Kyle, who were playing with a puppy speckled like a pig. Nora was laughing. I went over and squatted down next to them. "Hey, sillies," I said. "What's going on?"

"Dad needs a dog," Kyle said. He was petting the puppy as if he knew what he was doing, as though he'd grown up with dogs, which he hadn't. His round little face was solemn.

"Maybe you'll find him one," I said, and he smiled at me crookedly, which made me a little sad. Kyle had terrible teeth. I stood up.

"Look," Jilly said. She was holding the torn-ear dog on a lead made of braided plastic, like the lanyards we used to make in Girl Scout camp. "Barbie here says we can take this handsome young fellow for a walk. She's making an exception for us. You guys want to come with?"

"Sure," I said. I helped put the speckled puppy back in his cage, and took the kids' hands. We walked outside behind Jilly and the dog, whose name was Buck. "You can change his name," the smock woman called after us. She was warming up to us, I could tell.

Outside, the light was hard, glaring off the cars and picking out diamonds in the sidewalks. I looked down at the kids, who were holding my hands, kind of skipping along in unison, and I told them, "We'll get ice cream after." Jilly smiled, and I felt suddenly good about the afternoon, with its glare of heat. I had a friend. Her son was kind to the daughter I loved more than anything. I smiled back.

Jilly was at least 50 pounds overweight, and we'd only gone a block or two before she started puffing a little. "I could use a drink," she said. She handed me the leash while she mopped at her forehead. The braided plastic wasn't even pulled tight, but I could feel Buck's energy through it, a sort of humming tension. The dog had his dignity, I'll give him that. He walked almost pertly, without putting any real strain on the leash, which now that we were outside I could see was not really up to a dog his size.

"Isn't that Toy Train's house?" Jilly said.

"We should probably stop calling him that," I said. I switched Buck's leash to the other hand. "Good Boy," I told him. He looked up at me, grinning. By now he was panting almost as hard as Jilly.

"We should get Buck some water, too," I said, and nodded at the house, because there we were. It was, unsurprisingly, better kept than my own or Jilly's. Between the flagstone steps leading up to the front door, the grass was trimmed close as velvet. I had an image of Toy Train's mother down on her knees, snipping with scissors after the sun went down.

Jilly snorted. "She'll be thrilled to see us."

We started up the flagstone walk anyway. "Where are we going?" Kyle asked, and Nora echoed him. "Where are we going?"

"We're getting some water for Buck," I said. "This is Davey's house."

"Oh good!" Nora said. She smiled, innocent of her place in the play group hierarchy, and Kyle ran ahead and rang the bell.

But Toy Train's mother had already appeared at the door, and was looking at us through the screen as we stopped in the shade of the overhang. Jilly was making blowing noises, her sleeveless shirt wet under the arms in deep rings. I lifted my hair away from my neck and smiled.

"Hi there!" I said. "Remember us? Play group?" Toy Train's mom tilted her head noncommittally. "We were wondering if we could get a glass of water. We got this dog from the shelter." I waved my hand at Buck. "We're giving him a test drive, and we didn't reckon on the heat."

Toy Train pushed up from behind his mother and stared at us. He was holding a half sandwich with a few bites out of it, but when he saw Buck he stopped chewing. "Is that your dog?" he said through the food in his mouth. He pointed with the sandwich.

"Maybe," Kyle said. "He needs a drink."

Toy Train stuffed what was left of his sandwich into his mouth and opened the screen door.

His mother put a firm hand on his shoulder. "There's a hose out back for the dog," she said.

She tipped her head to the left, and Toy Train came outside. He jumped off the porch and Kyle and Nora followed him, all three of them disappearing around the corner of the house. Toy Train's mother just kept standing there. I finally nodded and made my way down the porch steps after the kids; as soon as I tugged the leash Buck got up and followed me. Jilly trailed behind.

Nora and Kyle and Toy Train were waiting for us when we got into the back yard. It was a lovely space, cool and green. Lots of trees: old-growth oaks and a few slippery elms. Davey, who was really a sweet little boy, had brought out a plastic cereal bowl. He put it under the spigot and then just looked up, puzzled.

"I've got it," I said. "Thank you, honey." Jilly, her face white, sat down in a deck chair, and I handed her Buck's leash. I filled the plastic bowl and set it down by Buck, who drank it all in a few slobbery gulps. I filled the bowl again. When I looked up, Davey's mother was standing on the patio with us, arms crossed over her chest. She looked at Jilly.

"Would you like a glass of water?"

Jilly nodded and the woman disappeared back into the house. I peered through the sliding door after her and I could see what was probably the family room. There was a toy train set up, and I wondered if they had to do that, what with the advertising and all. But everything was neat as a pin and for a moment I could see how that might be nice. I opened the door and stuck my head inside.

The air conditioning was on and it felt good, all right; I longed, suddenly, for this woman to know my worth. I stepped into the room and was almost next to the train table when Davey's mother came in from the kitchen. She stopped and stared when she saw me.

"Can I help?" I said, abashed. She handed me a juice glass; ice bobbed in the water.

"You have a beautiful house," I said, and she nodded.

"We added this room on last year," she said. "I had to convince my husband to do it — I mean, it's not like we needed the room!" She smiled quickly and looked out at the yard, at the kids, who were playing some sort of skipping game. "Well, you know how these things go. It was *so* disruptive! And of course *way* over budget!"

"I *know*," I said, and then we both laughed. I told her how we'd redone our bathroom right after we'd moved in. I may have embellished a little; at one point, the story had me wearing an overcoat out of the shower because I couldn't find my robe. But Davey's mother laughed again. She was entertained.

"This room, it's been worth the trouble," she said. "Davey and I spend a lot of time here; it's nice."

"Do you think I could have some water, too?" I asked then. My throat was so dry.

"In the kitchen." Davey's mother gestured, still looking out at the yard. "Glasses are in the cabinet over the sink. I'll just keep an eye on things here."

The kitchen was cool and dim, but the granite countertops had sparkles in them and trusted, free, I felt ridiculously happy. I opened the cabinet, and there, with the spices and a stack of mixing bowls, was a prescription bottle for something. I leaned closer. The orange plastic of that bottle glowed like a jewel in the half light. I still don't know for sure but I'm pretty sure it was Prozac. I'm pretty sure the bottle said Elizabeth. Elizabeth: Davey's mother's name was Beth, I remembered then, and I closed the cabinet and what I thought was that maybe we could, after all, be friends. In the next cabinet over were the glasses, and I chose a humble one. Thick blue glass. My favorite color. And I thought that this could be *my* glass, "Micky's glass." If we came again. To play trains, say.

When I rejoined Beth in the family room, we stood next to one another and looked outside. The kids were playing on a swing set in the back yard; Nora was swinging dreamily, her feet tucked. She said something to Davey and the boy nodded enthusiastically. "Your daughter is very well behaved," Beth said, and I beamed. "And how do you know Jillian?" she said then.

"Jilly? From group." My eyes moved from the kids to Jilly, who filled her chair, the roll of flesh showing beneath the hem of her tee shirt an almost shocking white. I glanced back at Beth, but her face was impossible to read.

"Let's get your friend her water," is what she said. When we got outside, I handed the cup to Jilly, who drained it in one swig.

"Is that dog safe?" Beth said. She had come up beside me and now she nodded at Buck, who was sprawled out on the cool patio tiles by Jilly's chair. He lifted his head when she said that; it was big as a box.

"Safe as houses," Jilly said.

"You have to be careful with dogs like that." Beth had been fussing with her hair, which was in a big sort of messy bun, and now she gave it a pat.

"We're just trying him out," I said.

"Trying him *out*," she echoed.

Jilly narrowed her eyes. "You like dogs, Beth?" Her face had some color back in it.

I looked at her: I'd never heard her use Beth's given name. She said it a certain way—just that one syllable, an exhalation.

"I'm not what you'd call a dog person."

"My mama always said not to trust anyone who doesn't like dogs," Jilly said. Now I just stared; she'd never, in all our conversations, called her mother "mama."

"Thanks for the water," I said then. I kept my voice relaxed, even smiling. This is the point where I would have gotten up to leave, but I was already standing: Beth hadn't offered me a chair. I looked at Jilly meaningfully. She gazed back at me placidly. The kids had wandered farther into the back yard together.

Beth turned away from Jilly to watch them. Nora was squatted down next to Davey. He was a blond kid. Tall and sturdy-looking, he was solicitous of my daughter, pointing at something out on the little pond behind his mother's house. Kyle stood off to the side. I know that look he had, because I have worn it myself.

Beth swung around abruptly. "That's a nice color on you, Michelle," she said. "With your eyes." She nodded at my shirt, which had a kangaroo pocket and was a brilliant shade of blue. In fact I'd bought it because of the color, but right now it was sticking to my back, crumpled from the heat.

"Thanks," I said, but Beth had already turned to Jilly.

"Your husband is in law enforcement, Jillian?"

"Oh, call me Jilly," Jilly said. "I ain't much for airs."

"He's a police officer? Jilly?"

"He's a cop. Yeah." Jilly's voice had taken on the flat, dangerous edge it sometimes got just before she started yelling at the kids.

"Nora!" I called. My daughter looked at me pleadingly. She was having fun out there, just a stone's throw from a real backyard pond. "Time to head out!"

Buck pricked up his ears and stood also, but Jilly just kept on sitting there. "I'll get the kids," I said.

"Don't you worry?" Beth said to Jilly. "With all the things one hears—"

"Oh, Doug can take care of himself," I said quickly, before Jilly could answer. The conversation suddenly felt risky, on the edge of meanness or stupidity or both.

"Never mind," Jilly said, looking at me. "It doesn't matter."

"No, I guess it really doesn't," Beth said.

I turned back to the yard. "Nora Ann!"

Kyle was already halfway to the patio, relief on his face. But Nora and Davey hadn't budged.

"I'll just go get them," I said.

"Davey!" Beth yelled. "*Now!*" It was as if she'd unleashed an electric current: both Davey and Nora turned as one, and without even looking at each other started trotting back to the patio. Later I tried to ask Nora about it. "It was time to *go*, Mom," was all she said.

They were still almost-running when they got to the patio. I don't really know exactly what happened next, except that one moment Buck was standing next to Jilly, and the next he was on top of Davey. He wasn't growling or snapping; I think to this day that he was playing. All I know is that the kid started screaming. Beth paused for a shocked millisecond before she yelled at the dog. Then she yelled at Jilly. The dog started barking. Davey was crying. And Beth took one of those deck chairs and let Buck have it.

What can I say? It was pandemonium. Nora had started crying too, and Beth was still yelling, swinging that chair while Jilly just shook her head in wonder. Was she laughing? She might have been. Buck took off, his leash trailing behind him like a rainbow.

"Everyone calm down," I yelled, but no one listened to me, except for maybe Nora, who came and buried her face in my side.

"I want to go home, Mama," she said.

The chair lay in splinters on the grass. Beth leaned over and scooped up her son; it was amazing, what such a tiny woman could do. "It's time for you to leave," she said then. Her voice was almost level but her hair had come undone. It swept across her cheek like a gash, and I knew, looking at her fine-featured face, that nothing like this was ever supposed to happen to someone like her.

"The leash just slipped out of my hand," Jilly shrugged.

"I'm sorry about the dog," I said, steering Nora past Jilly, who had finally stood up. "I'm really sorry." I stopped in front of Beth, who held Davey tight. He was scrubbing at his face with a dirty hand and hiccupping. One of Buck's nails had scratched his cheek. "You okay, honey?"

"He's fine," Jilly pronounced, sweeping past me. She had one hand on Kyle's shoulder.

"Let me know if you need anything," I said to Beth.

"*Michelle*, we have to go find Buck," Jilly said. She was at the corner of the house now, fists on her hips.

"I'm sorry," I said again, but Beth straightened up and looked past me, at Jilly. It was like I wasn't even there.

"Better shake a leg," Jilly said.

I turned away from Beth, and from Davey, who hung on his mother's leg now.

"Yeah, better shake a leg," I heard then, from behind me, and I knew it wasn't Davey, with his corn-yellow hair. I knew it wasn't Davey: that cruel, mincing voice.

We scoured the neighborhood for Buck and only found him when we returned to the shelter, defeated. He'd come back the hour before and was already safe in his kennel. We made our apologies to Barb, whose hostility was impossible to ignore.

"Are we bringing Buck home?" Kyle asked.

"I don't think so," Jilly said.

We got the kids back into the car. They reminded me that I'd promised ice cream and because I was too tired to say no, I took them all to Dairy King. Everyone was silent in the car, and we were silent in line at Dairy King, where the kids got twist cones and Jilly ordered something called a peanut belly burst. I asked for water. My head was killing me, and I was sick of the sweets I only ate when I was with Jilly.

There was a little park at Dairy King: a set of swings and a sand pit that you just knew feral cats pissed in on a routine basis. "Stay out of the sand," I said. Nora gave me a look, but both she and Kyle went to sit on the jungle gym.

I returned to Jilly, who sprawled on a bench that was partway out of the sun. She stared at me, spooning ice cream into her mouth. "You were really rude," I said.

"She's a bitch," Jilly said dismissively.

I stuck my hands in the kangaroo pocket of my shirt. It really was a nice shade of blue. "She did give you water. You could at least be polite."

"Why?" Jilly asked. "I'd rather be real." She set the empty ice cream cup down and stretched her arms over her head; I saw how heavy they were. I glanced down at her tee shirt, which was riding up again.

"Your stomach's showing," I said.

If I was another kind of woman, I'd have stayed friends with Jilly forever. If Jilly was another kind of woman, she would have lost weight, and our two families would have gone hiking together, in a distant land. Yellowstone, say, where we would have run rings around the hot pots. My mother's cancer would go into remission, and she'd be there to console me when Nora hit her teens. She'd be there for Nora's graduation, and so would Jilly, because Jilly and Doug and Kyle would be like family. Kyle, with his round merciful face and earthbound patience.

That's what might've happened. But in the end? The play group wrapped up when summer came. Jilly and I tried to meet for lunch a few times, with the kids, but it never seemed to come together; when Nora started kindergarten I went back to work. A person gets busy.

Nora never got invited to Davey's house, but if it bothered her she never let on. She eventually skipped second grade and graduated high school early. Along the way she managed to make a couple friends, enough to get through. I hear Kyle was the same, though the two of them traveled in different circles. Kyle wasn't a theater kid. I think he did sports.

I'd see Jilly in passing, but even in a small town, a person can disappear. The kids were in college already when we ran into one another at J.C. Penney, at the Ephrem Mall. She hadn't changed that much; in the manner of those who are overweight, she looked younger in the face, probably younger than I did anymore. We talked about the kids—Nora was at Claremont McKenna. Kyle was going to the state school across the Wisconsin border, and it was clear Jilly was proud of him.

"You working?" I asked. I didn't mean anything by it. I have a job with the city, writing press releases full time. I like the work. The people there are my friends now. I had come straight from the office when I saw Jilly, and I was dressed for it: a skirt and heels, but low ones. A nice tweed blazer that I'd splurged on when I first got the job. She looked me up and down but said nothing; her tee shirt had that yellow Pikachu on it.

"Anyway," I said, and waited. I guess I thought that after all these years she was finally going to tell me something.

"How's your mom?" she said then. My mom had died years ago. A lifetime ago, it felt like; I remember Jilly sending flowers when Mom was so ill, but the kind in a pot, that weren't supposed to die.

I gazed at Jilly, her rounded cheeks, pitted like a breadfruit. That pillar of hair. Her life had gone on without me, and mine without her.

Then I thought about what Nora sometimes says, which is that I take things too much to heart. My daughter loves me. So does Ben.

"Mom died a long time ago, Jilly," I told her. "It's been years."
I tried to say it gentle.

"I'm sorry," Jilly said. Which is what people say. She shifted
her purse, a great baggy thing, to her other shoulder.

Or as people also say, Whatever.

PANTHEISM

My grandmother appears
     as Spinoza: skin gaunt

as parchment, the landscape
     granular behind her. *We need*

to leave Poland now. She points
     to the holes in her face, presses

her palms as prayer into her ribs.
     Somehow I can feel this

pressure on my chest.
     Years later, I think I find her

eyes blooming in the desert.
     Mine itch. Whose rifle rankles

my skin? On the other side
     of the razor fence, I see a woman

with my grandmother's face. She throws stones
     and shouts my name.

LOVE POEM AFTER 10 YEARS

Post-take off, a younger woman presses
      her luminous mouth to the glass and laughs

nervously. We're far from safe ground. It's hot,
      my palms sweat, our thighs keep

touching. Once I was in love like that. Afloat,
      sun-struck. I want to tear a lock of her

hair because it's healthy and I'm not
      ready to spiral through this plunging city

grey and thinning. Before you, I was
      a means of transportation: private jet,

shimmering pulley. Sometimes I was not
      luxurious thing but absent life form:

worm regenerating and torn, girl dragging
      the leash of her pretend dog. Before you,

I was miserable with no words for love-
      making. That wasn't love. These years I've no

proof of love other than what our bodies do.
      I've lost my grandmother's ring, so many

animals to the clouds, an imagined
      child. Now we are a sinking life-

boat pulled toward the blue, where we try to
      breathe. I'm the rip current, and

you're the diver. From the depths, reach up and
      grab the star between my thighs.

ABDUCTIONS

Some summer nights I felt called to go outside.
With sequins of stars loosening in the sky,
I scanned all points from north to south, east to west.
      Twinkly as before,
the night didn't hint at a star that might turn
into a spacecraft, round as a plate a-glow,
rainbow-colored, softly blinking and swooping
      down without a hum,
with not a wide window like on *Lost in Space*,
with not an underside door open-tonguing
unleashing a green laser beam to zap me
      into submission.
There, I'd be beamed up, strangely floating like a wisp
onto a table, feeling a rush of chill
across my body as their almond-downward
      eyes stayed unblinking.
The mucus-gray color of their skin would throb
eerily like a mood ring as they come close,
their narrow shoulders and small bodies would seem
      improbably frail
to support their enormous heads. But their eyes:
not a flicker of emotion or question,
just like how my doctor gazed at me before
      the anesthesia
kicked in. His eyes hovered above the white mask.
He asked how I was feeling but I didn't
know this. I couldn't lipread through his fabric.
      His masked attendants

hovered nearby as I tried to resist the
urge to fall asleep. I'd spotted the trays of
surgical instruments shiny and ready
      as if for dinner.
He was to probe my right ear and see if he
could make it hear better. No one explained
just what would be done to me on that morning.
      I had to trust him
totally like how Mom trusted our quiet priest,
Father Frank, who was impossible to read
on the lips; his Sunday babble made no sense.
      I lay white-sheeted,
feeling slightly chilled, as if the aliens
had entered the operating room as ghosts,
hovering as my mind's ear caught the static
      from their own language;
they seemed to be debating whether I should
be taken along to wherever they lived . . .
Then I woke up to find Mom smiling,
      asking how I'd felt.
Not long after, when I became more alert,
my doctor anxiously smiled as I put in
my earmold to see if I could detect a
      change in my hearing.
None at all. My audiologist confirmed
it was still the same. That winter night I looked
up to the stars, yearning for the aliens
      to take me away.
There had to be a better planet where I
didn't have to feel like an alien, mute
with the ache for communication so clear
      I could touch the stars.

I've heard horror stories about hungry
pets and their dead owners . . .

WHAT HAPPENS NEXT

A few days after I decided not to kill myself, my cat, Harold, shat on my bed. This sweet orange tabby—a cat who charmed nearly everyone, even the allergic and the feline intolerant—had a tendency to do this when I let his litter box go a few too many days without changing. I took the box outside to dump it in the trash, pungent ammonia-reek of cat piss wafting from the can along with something nasty already rotting there. It was a dark, cloud-covered day and I was feeling a creeping anxiety as I waited for the time to pass so that I could go to the composition class I was teaching. It was my first semester and standing in front of a class of twenty students still gave me a jolt of surreal fear as if they saw something that my mirror wasn't giving away each morning, something bad. What were they looking at? What did they want from me?

"I just realized this morning that I was no longer thinking of death as a passive event," I said to Curt as we walked around the University of Tennessee campus. *"Gee, if a bus would just run me down, all my problems would be solved. Or maybe cancer. Maybe cancer wouldn't be so bad.* I've been thinking that killing myself could be a distinct possibility. I think I can do this."

The above is probably more concise than what actually came out. It was one thing to lie in bed for hours, staring at the dingy chandelier (three uncovered bulbs glowing, one burnt black, the other missing, a spider web strand hanging from the lamp chain, another blown sideways by the heating vents), planning my death down to what I would do with my cats (I couldn't very well leave them if I was planning to shoot myself in the head — they might be scared by the dead body in the tub. Or, worse, I might not be discovered for weeks — I've heard horror stories about hungry pets and their dead owners . . .) and it was another thing to speak these plans out loud. While contemplating suicide that morning, I had also considered telling friends of my plans in case they might want to talk me out of it. I imagined giving different versions of these impassioned, eloquent, suffering speeches. I'd be bitter, yes, waving a sad farewell to this life, maybe even a bit angry. But it was another thing to actually hear these words aloud. I stammered. I paused for minutes at a time as I searched for the inadequate words which would convey what I was convinced were really crucial and complex thoughts. I repeated myself. I said things that I later realized I didn't mean. As I told my friend Curt my plans, tried to articulate my thoughts, I slowly became aware of what was the strongest feeling swirling around this maelstrom of emotion: embarrassment.

My first fiction writing teacher in college told me not to talk about stories before writing. "Just do it. If you talk about a story, that takes the place of writing it." I believe that this is true. But one thing he didn't tell, which I would later learn (because, of course, I didn't follow his advice): Stories that haven't been written almost always sound really stupid. And when you hear your stupid story coming out of your mouth and see your friends trying to nod encouragingly, you know for a fact that you're never going to write this idiot tale.

It was cringe-worthy hearing my suicidal thoughts out loud as Curt and I walked around campus on this spring-like January day. Everyone wants to think that their experiences and thoughts are unique and I'm no different. I wasn't a goth teen or middle-aged alcoholic; my suicidal thoughts were original. But I was a writer and there was no way to ignore the banal and clichéd sounds I was making. I couldn't even look my friend in the face.

I was obsessed with time, constantly checking my watch, looking at every clock, measuring the sand fall with greedy fingers. *There goes another wasted minute. Where did it go? What did I do with it?* This obsession was both anxiety-producing and incredibly boring. Time was one dull moment followed by another, dissatisfaction an almost palpable presence. I was too much with my thoughts, too much in my skull.

When one thinks of killing oneself, the very first question is naturally, *What do you have to complain about?* I was a writer who could spend much of my day writing and reading. I was a college instructor, a guy my landlord referred to as "the professor" to the other tenants although I was just an adjunct. I played in a band that had just released a CD. I had no disabilities, had not been sick in over a year, had not lost any of my immediate family to death, drugs, or dementia, and it was a beautiful day to boot. What did I have to complain about?

To the non-suicidal, it is difficult to explain, but when you think of nothing but what is negative in life, when you are weighed down by the thought that nothing is worth doing, and pleasure is a vague memory, when you are paralyzed with the realization that this is the best it will ever get, when you can't help but think *If only I just stopped existing, the pain, the monotonous pain would end,* then the next question after *What do you have to complain about?* is *Can you kill yourself?* Always, in the past, the answer had been *No.* Then one day, with mild surprise, I answered *Yes.*

I instinctively knew that I had to succeed, that to fail at suicide was one of the worst kinds of failures a guy can have. I had a roommate in college who attempted to kill himself. He slashed his arm and went to his ex-girlfriend's house so that she could simultaneously feel guilt for driving him to this end and bandage him up. He was institutionalized and I visited him in the mental ward of a hospital where depressed teens shot pool and wandered the hallways and an old man had a shrieking d.t. episode in which he hallucinated bugs as if to demonstrate how bad things could get. My friend's mother arrived from out of town to clean our — her — filthy house, cut the overgrown yard, and promptly evict all his roommates. There seemed to be something shameful about surviving a suicide attempt, something messy and unclean.

Here is what I would do:

I would board my cats at the vet and then go to a sporting goods shop and purchase a gun. At the gun shop I would be sure to tell the salesperson that I knew nothing about guns, but lived in a high-crime neighborhood and wanted something that would "stop" an intruder, not wound him. I might wink and say, "If you know what I mean." The salesperson *would* know what I meant, would show me how to load the gun, operate it. At home, I would leave a brief message in my landlord's mailbox, telling him to call the police and come down to unlock the door for them, but *not* to come in the apartment himself. I'd go home. Perhaps, I'd dress up — coat and tie — this part is a little fuzzy. I would leave simple instructions: cremate me, give away my few belongings. I would want my cats to live with my ex-wife because they knew and loved her.

Then I would climb in the bathtub to make cleanup easier. I would raise the barrel to my temple, remind myself that the innate will to survive is powerful, that many people have lived through this type of suicide attempt, that despite all good intentions, some pull the gun away at the last second, send the bullet into their nose or through their jaw or graze their brain, making them instant circus freaks or vacant-eyed droolers. Best bet: put the bullet in the center of the brain — a hot piece of lead makes it difficult to think negative thoughts and, consequently, to walk, eat, live.

My therapist, Mike, was not shocked by my plan. In fact, in our late-afternoon session, he looked a little sleepy. He'd probably heard this story many times.

"You're obviously very angry at your ex-wife."

"What?" This is not what I was talking about. I was talking

about blowing my brains out.

"That's what I'm hearing."

I wrinkled my forehead in thought, reflected. I was not convinced.

Sometime in the mid-nineties, I lived with a woman who would become my wife. We shared the top floor of a Victorian house with hardwood floors, an old washing machine which vibrated the silverware and dishes, a drier which frosted the windows, and a back door leading down steep steps where our cats would run in and out during warm weather. Years after my divorce, selective memory sometime let me think of those days as halcyon, untroubled by more than the occasional disagreement (the checkbook entries should take two lines instead of one, I cut the grass last time so it's your turn, etc.). She managed a health food store, I, a used book and CD store — our main necessities at the tips of our fingers: food, music, literature. She wrote poetry, I, fiction. We rode our bikes to the swimming pool or lay in the sun in our backyard. We ate dinner together and sat and talked as the kitchen and dining room dimmed. Sometimes, she sat on my lap, arms around my neck, lips to my razor-stubbled chin.

The summer after we married, the city decided to repave the street in front of our house, a main thoroughfare. About time, we and several of our neighbors said; it had been pocked with potholes for years. Early one morning, workers came riding heavy machinery which scooped up pavement with great, shrieking sounds. The trolley tracks which had been covered up sometime earlier in the century saw light, emerging from the pavement like subconscious thought. It was quaint to see those two lines revealed, to think of people riding a train car down our street, boys hanging off, shouting at the people in the houses. But then the workers disappeared for no apparent reason, tractors abandoned at the end of the street like outgrown toys. The gray dirt from beneath the pavement floated in the air, sticking to our clothes and skin, touching our tongues with chalk. Every time I had to drive across the tracks, I gritted my teeth, waiting for the crunch of metal against the belly of my little Nissan.

Several months later, the night before Thanksgiving, my wife came home and said she wanted to split up. She was obsessed with the tennis pro at the gym where she was now teaching aerobics, unsure if she found me attractive anymore, unsure if she loved me.

"How could you not know I was unhappy?" she wanted to know. "What did you think was going on?"

Although we didn't separate that night, we did about a year later. The night my wife and I finally decided to take the plunge, I spent over an hour on the phone with each of my parents. I'm not the most communicative person, especially not with my parents, so this news blindsided them. They thought we were happy. "Have you tried counseling?" my father wanted to know. (We had.) "How long have you known there were problems?" (A while.) "Who asked for the divorce?" (She did.) "Have one of you been having an affair?" The questions kept coming. Surely, I thought, divorce was not such a baffling mystery. I felt as if I had failed my family, as if I had killed myself, but remained able to use the phone so that I could attempt to explain my senseless act to the survivors.

My father is a good talker. My mother was more like me, taciturn, unsure about what to say on the phone. There was the occasional "Well." There was "I don't know what to say" or "This is such a surprise." Then Mom said, "I wish you were here, so I could hold you, just sit and hold you." Twenty years later, those words are moving to write. But at the time they were a burden. I had so clearly disappointed everyone, had failed once again. I had dropped out of college—twice—had been caught smoking pot in high school several times, had driven a car into a building, but this was the worst. I had invited this person into our life, given my parents a new daughter, and then I had to tell them that it wasn't working out, that this daughter was going to go away and they'd never see her again. There were no words. I wanted to get down on all fours like an animal and crawl under a piece of furniture where it would be dark and cool. I wanted to close my eyes, breathe slow with the deep pulls from my chest, ribcage shifting like some piece of medieval machinery, a perpetual motion machine sucking and spitting air.

My parents divorced when I was about seven and the only memories I have of them together is while fighting. Here's one:

My father comes home and enters the kitchen. He and my mother stand at opposite ends of the room speaking in tense tones, faces tight with some mysterious pressure. Suddenly, my father grabs an egg from the countertop and throws it into the sink, yelling, "Goddamnit!" My mother's reaction to this baffling behavior is sudden and electric: "You son-of-a-bitch! I spend all day cleaning this house and you . . ." and she is on him like a feral cat. He grabs her by the wrists and they struggle. This is terrifying from the floor-view of a toddler. I will remember it forever.

And yet, I'm sure my parents have other stories. In fact, I do too. I remember our family taking a summer trip to Bluffton, SC to visit my father's sister and her family at their summer home. My parents were together. And surely, they didn't fight because this perfect memory isn't tainted at all.

I remember pretending to be superheroes with my siblings and cousins down by the river. I remember pulling up wooden traps full of live crabs onto my aunt and uncle's dock. I remember breaking the shells of those crabs, still hot from the steamer, eating their flesh, even the yellow guts. I remember learning to pry open clams, dipping their gelatinous interiors in red sauce and letting them slide down my throat. I remember watching the adults play tennis and tiptoeing barefooted across the hot asphalt to pull a soft drink from a cooler, wondering how 7-Up could taste so much better out here by the river. I remember being amazed that, though my puppy, George, had never seen a body of water, he could swim just as well as my cousins' dog who lived by the river.

And I remember being stripped naked after a day in the sun, wet and warm beneath my aunt and uncle's outdoor shower, bathing suit replaced by a strip of white, stark against the dark brown my skin had become. My siblings, cousins, and I, too young to be ashamed by our nakedness, took turns stepping beneath the stream of water, passed a bar of soap around. My uncle walked down the line, squirting a blob of shampoo into each of our upturned hands. "Don't worry," he assured us, "it's tearless." As I rubbed the shampoo into my scalp and it dripped down my forehead and ran across my eyeballs, I didn't blink.

"That fucking bitch" my sister would often say in regards to my ex-wife. She was a lot angrier than I was, though I would be lying if I claimed I didn't get pleasure from her words. Still, I continued to socialize with my ex-wife — go out for beers, feed her cats when she was out of town — for the entire two years after our divorce when we lived in the same town, while she dated first the tennis pro, then a mutual acquaintance, then some guy I didn't know. Mike, my therapist, said I was experiencing anger vicariously through my sister.

He regarded me, eyebrows moving together. "Do you *ever* feel rage?"

I cogitated, stared at the ceiling to demonstrate my consideration of this question. "No, I don't think so."

But maybe I'm too hasty with this response. Once, when I was fifteen, I had a run-in with my mother before school, a little disagreement over something which quickly became frightening.

My mother was not a good listener generally, cut me off mid-sentence. Usually, I would shut down and let her talk. But sometimes, like on that morning, I would shout over her in order to be heard.

When I shouted, she raised her voice above mine, screamed

"Don't talk back to me!" and slapped me across the face as hard as she could. She had hit me many times before, but never in the face. There's something humiliating about being hit in the face and I reacted without thinking, swung my fist, knuckles clenched. I stopped, fist inches away, and then walked out of the house. We never spoke about this incident.

My neighbor in my first apartment after the divorce was a good old boy, also divorced, also betrayed by a wife. We would sit on our shared porch and drink and commiserate about our unluckiness in love. He had had suicidal thoughts too, had wanted to "suck a gun." But he said, "You can't do that because you know why? They win." His jaw dropped when I told him I was on friendly terms with my ex. He took a swig of beer and pointed the bottle at me, eyes dark and serious, lower lip protruding — a perpetual cup for tobacco even when not dipping. "Your psychiatrist is right. You gotta feel rage. You gotta get pissed. My wife ran off to Kentucky with another guy, but I stayed in the house because you know why? I knew she'd be back. I came home from work one day and there she was. I just walked through the house smashing everything in sight. The table — *Pow!* — up against the wall. I picked up the TV — *Smash!* I didn't care what I did. She was crying and scared, but I said, 'I've never hit a woman and I don't mean to start now. Just count yourself lucky, bitch.' And then I walked out of that house and never went back." He measures me with his eyes. "That's probably not your style, but buddy, you got to do something. Embarrass her publicly. I wouldn't mind doing it for you. I can walk into her work and just start cussing: 'You goddamned whore. You'll suck any dick within five feet of your face. Why, I wouldn't fuck your pussy with the dick of a dead man.' Or trash her car. She'll never know it was you, but you'll be able to feel better about this situation."

I laughed, not really at what he was saying, but at the absurdity that I could actually be a part of any such activity. Still, the thought of vandalizing her car did have its appeal. I could imagine the warm wood of a baseball bat in my hand, dull thud of safety glass — stubbornly holding together even as it dents inward, spider web cracks crawling across its surface — crunch of glass shards beneath rubber soles. I know my neighbor was imagining a stealthy attack — vandalism committed in black clothing, shoe polish on the face. But once the sound filled my ears, once I felt the give of solid surfaces beneath my hands, I wouldn't stop. Police officers would say, "Sir, drop the bat and put your hands in the air!" They would have to drag me from that car grasping the window, glass biting into my hand. *That's okay, an experience like this deserves a souvenir I can carry in my palm forever.*

Somehow, though, I know I'll never experience any of the above moments. Something keeps me behaving the way people who know me expect me to behave.

It took me seven years, but I found someone, a woman I met in grad school, who I wanted to be with for the rest of my life. She and I have been married for over a decade, so this is the longest romantic relationship of my life as I pass the age of fifty. After years of therapy and writing and more soul-searching than could be interesting for any reader, I have learned to feel rage. Sometimes to scary effect. My wife and I have thrown things. We scream at each other so that I wonder what the neighbors think. We have been seen by a friend in the streets of Brooklyn fighting, not once, but twice. And yet, we always make up, we always put our arms around each other before bed. We say the words "I love you" multiple times a day.

I take 30 milligrams of Lexapro every morning. But I'm convinced that this, alone, isn't what has kept me alive. I believe that the love my wife feels for me, and that I feel for her, is the crux of the matter. My mother never remarried although she was an attractive woman in her thirties after my parents' divorce and at least four men over the years asked her to marry them, despite the fact that she came with the three kids of another man. After a certain point, men stopped asking her.

About fifteen years ago—coincidentally, the same year that I met my second wife—my mother attempted suicide. She swallowed all the painkillers she'd been on for the previous year for chronic back pain. After a fevered phone call from my sister and an outrageously expensive "bereavement flight," I was next to my mother's hospital bed where we were informed by a distracted doctor that she might or might not survive. The next twenty-four hours would tell. Mom looked like an insect or, more apt, something left over after an insect has finished sucking out the insides. She was thin as bone from starving herself for the months prior to the attempt, skin waxy with the scent and look of death. There was a big tube running into her nose where she was being force-fed liquids. She managed to open sticky lips and say, "I'm sorry, honey. The Parkinson's had just gotten too bad."

A couple months prior to this attempt, Mom had been diagnosed with Parkinson's and the week before, her mother had had a stroke and was hospitalized, paralyzed over half of her body. Although my grandmother had been living on her own a block away from my mother's, she was in her upper nineties and no longer drove. My mother was responsible for driving my grandmother to doctor's appointments, taking her to the grocery store, sometimes cooking for her. The night before my mother's suicide attempt, due to the stiffening of her joints from the Parkinson's, she almost wrecked her car coming home from the hospice where my grandmother was convalescing. She was overwhelmed and wanted out.

After she was out of danger, in a moment when she and I were alone in her hospital room together, feeding tube no longer shoved up a nostril, a more human pallor to her skin, she said these words to me: "Men no longer look at me."

Of all the things she could say to me no more than forty-eight hours after her near successful suicide attempt, this was one of the more perplexing ones and for years I had no idea why she spoke them. But I'm getting closer to figuring out what she was trying to say.

She was alone. Her kids had all moved away. Her mother's problems had become too big for her to deal with (luckily, my grandmother had another daughter who could step in and take care of her for her next several years of her life). Mom knew that once the mess of her life was arranged to our satisfaction, that we would leave Florida and go back to our lives in Alabama, West Virginia, Nebraska.

Although my mother rallied briefly after the suicide attempt, moved to Alabama to be closer to her only grandchild, even bought a house, she still needed a daily pill, like her son, to keep from killing herself. In addition, she went through several sessions of electroconvulsive therapy and was institutionalized to avoid hurting herself more than once. After a few years, she deteriorated to the point where she couldn't take care of herself, let alone kill herself if she had wanted to, though she once asked a nurse to help her do the deed. For over a decade, we watched my mother die in slow motion which she finally finished doing, dying in her sleep a couple months ago.

I am not going to say that people shouldn't kill themselves. Coming from me of all people that would be the height of hypocrisy. There is probably some gene in my lineage that makes this a compelling act. My mother's brother killed himself in his twenties (the family story, for years, was that it was a hunting accident). I always found this uncle — who I remember only vaguely for bringing me a gift of plastic dinosaurs when I was a child — a mysterious, ghostly presence in my life. I discovered a Spiro Agnew watch in my mother's stuff that had apparently belonged to him. I still have it though it doesn't keep time. I never knew my uncle well enough to know if it appealed to him for its kitsch value or if he liked it unironically. Anyway, Western prohibitions about suicide are cultural not ethical, having to do with entrenched Judeo-Christian teachings and Protestant attitudes toward work ethic and suffering. In Japan and some other Eastern countries, writers, politicians and other public figures kill themselves and the action is not necessarily shameful, sometimes it's even admired. What I *am* going to suggest, though, is that great adversity—the diagnosis of a degenerative and incurable illness, a mother's massively debilitating stroke, the loneliness of a menopausal life, one's children living far away—is easier to bear when one has a life partner, someone who loves you more than anyone else in the world, someone who you can trust to be there in the morning when you awake, someone who will feed you when you're ill, who will caress and comfort you when you feel hopeless. I realize that there are many people out there who live happy lives by themselves, who don't need anyone else to give their lives meaning, and I am happy for them. But I am not one of them and I don't think my mother was either.

As I stood in front of my apartment in Knoxville, Tennessee, fetid reek rising from my garbage can, a shat-upon bed waiting for me inside, I was immersed in unpleasantness, a prime moment, I knew from experience, that could send me into a tailspin, obsessed by dark thoughts, wallowing in pessimism. But amidst my muttering curses and fantasies about what I might do to my cat if I were a different kind of person, the sun came out from behind the clouds and I was startled from my glowering for a scintillating moment as I realized that, despite the fact that it was mid-February, the ground around me was covered in bright, purple flowers—at least a hundred of them. It was startling, beautiful, and I stood there just looking, not thinking about how this probably had something to do with global warming, not thinking about my petty problems nor tormented by the tick of the clock, just being in the moment.

PANTOUM AS PROOF OF THE GENTLE

What a forbidden song.
The moment where we all sang together in perfect harmony
  passed so long ago.
It does not matter if I don't like the words I am saying; all that
  matters is that I am saying them.
The sea witch does not just capture the voice, but holds onto the
  entire mind.

The moment where we all sang together in perfect harmony
  passed so long ago.
A forgotten vibrato as the birds hold their notes as long as possible.
The sea witch does not just capture the voice, but holds onto the
  entire mind.
This is holy matrimony of the senses.

A forgotten vibrato as the birds hold their notes as long as possible.
Why does the bird only sing during the day?
This is holy matrimony of the senses.
Imagine the night lit up with the sounds of birdsong.

Why does the bird only sing during the day?
How lovely that would be against the graying light polluted sky.
Imagine the night lit up with the sounds of birdsong.
This is holy matrimony of the senses.

How lovely that would be against the graying light polluted sky.
What a forbidden song.
This is holy matrimony of the senses.
It does not matter if I don't like the words I am saying; all that
    matters is that I am saying them.

3 A.M. ONE-SIDED CONVERSATIONS WITH MARY

The Virgin Mary sleeps at
the foot of my bed, crosshatching
upon her face a suggestion of shadow.

Is it easier to find calm if you know
what lies ahead
is better than the present?

Have you ever seen the Pieta?
How the mother's hands grab her
son of stone and seem to sink in
at the very suggestion of softness.

This abstraction of ideality.
Oh Madonna, where does your serenity come from?
For I am struggling just to breath
and you hold onto the lifeless body of your own son.

Sad tearless eyes;
I might as well your fraternal stone,
the way this untouchable exhaustion weighs me down.
The half-ton of damp river rocks in my pockets

contradicts the unbearable lightness of
pink tinted saline, the runoff
of slab upon slab of Himalayan salt named sacred.

I pull at the weight bearing support
and the entire wooden scaffolding comes
crashing down around me.

How do you continue to carry yourself so tall through
life, the after, and the limitless space in between?
As if you have not been beaten down more times
than the number of fingers on hands and toes on feet

When you speak I picture a mountain range of femininity.
To weave beautiful fabric from the scrap pile of what remains,
    womanhood.

That morning the first thing I do
is buy my own burial plot.
I meet her eyes again and I swear
she winks.

Glory made sure her door was locked, put her
headphones back on, and switched the tape to side B.

GLORY UNDER QUARANTINE

On the day before Glory's fourteenth birthday party, China Spring Middle School had been closed for a week following Derrick Naylor's diagnosis with a particularly virulent strain of chlamydia, which he'd contracted the previous year and been too scared to tell anybody about. Untreated, it had metastasized, or whatever chlamydia does, and Derrick was at Scott & White now with an arsenal of scalpels and laser beams pointed at his groin. The *Waco Tribune Herald* ran Derrick's yearbook picture on the front page of the local section over a headline that read: "The Battle of His Life."

It was determined that the school would stay closed until every single student presented the office with a clean bill of sexual health.

Which meant Glory had stayed home all week while her grandmother was at work. She microwaved pizza rolls or soup and watched TV as game shows for stay-at-home white people become syndicated sitcoms with laugh tracks for nobody. It was the hottest February on record, or so said the radio, even though it looked like winter outside, all bare trees and stonewashed sky. The day before, she'd got a call from the school secretary who asked that all tokens of condolence be sent through the school. Didn't Glory maybe want to send Derrick a card or one of those supermarket balloons? No, thank you, Glory did not.

Nobody knew who'd made their chlamydia Derrick's. Junie, Glory's grandmother, had her suspicions. She pronounced all parties involved dyed-in-the-wool hoochies. Derrick must've known the culprit's identity, but he wasn't talking, Whoever it was, Glory knew — or she was beginning to understand — that she was the culprit behind the culprit. Everyone who crossed Glory, Glory destroyed.

After thorough deliberation, her grandmother decided to cancel Glory's birthday party, but she assured her that it was not a punishment.

"I didn't even invite any boys," Glory told her on the drive to the urgent clinic.

"You gotta read the tea leaves, honey," her grandmother replied. "Everybody's under lock and key. Your little friends wouldn't be allowed to come anyway."

Glory rolled the passenger window down. Her grandmother rolled it up. Sullenly, after the appropriate time for a reply had passed, Glory said, "You don't know that."

"You gotta take the temperature of the situation," her grandmother said. "Besides, you used to love birthdays with just me and your uncle Keith. It'll be like old times."

And that was all that was said about it. Junie paged backward through celebrity magazines in the waiting room while Glory's sexual health was appraised by an elderly doctor whose breath smelled like hot leather. When she returned to the waiting room, she only acknowledged her grandmother to snatch her car keys off the magazine table. A blur of tear-streaked cheeks and weathervane ponytail pointed toward general storminess. Behind her, the clinic door hydraulically moseyed shut.

From the car, Glory watched her grandmother waddle through the parking lot, crabwalking between the cars, using her cane less as an appurtenance than a dowsing rod. Her grandmother was half in the car when Glory asked her why she was so obsessed with ruining her life.

"What in the world are you talking about?" her grandmother asked. "You're clean as a whistle, no chlamydia, no nothing. At least so far as the doctor can tell."

Glory leaned her seat back and rolled her eyes at the baggy

blue ceiling fabric. "Oh my gosh," she said, "I'm so relieved."

"Well, Gloribelle, you should be. You can get herpes from a drinking fountain. You can be pure till your wedding night just like I was, but that don't mean you're safe. Not anymore. Not in this fallen world."

"I'm so lucky," Glory said. She ran her fingernail along the side of her seat, dislodging old booger encrustations. Like picking a scab, but grosser, and way less satisfying. "And I should be grateful too," she added, "shouldn't I? To have a grandmother who's totally obsessed with ruining my life."

"Good lord. You use that word too much," Junie said. "*Obsessed*. It makes you sound ignorant."

They arrived back home to find Glory's uncle in the midst of one of his tantrums. He was ransacking the pantry and the linen closet, looking for something he was too exasperated to name. Uncle Keith had been on disability for the last couple years after sliding down the roof of a Quonset hut into a truck bed full of lumber. He'd broken his hip, and the accident had destroyed his confidence in his ability not only to walk steadily atop Quonset hut roofs, of which his previous job had largely consisted, but to do manual labor in general. He languored, God bless him, signed his government checks over to his mother, slept into the afternoon, and upon waking, would continue where he left off the day before, designing a sequel to *The Oregon Trail*, in which the trail itself wound not only directionally, but metaphysically, westward, through time tunnels sprinkled with destinations in the historical past and the speculative future. During his long convalescence, the poor man had taken computer classes at the community college, taught himself video game design, read and reread Baudrillard's *Simulacra and Simulation* searching for clues pointing to his game's true essence. He'd breathed make-believe trail dust and space dust for the better part of two years, and all for naught, because today, he learned by post, the long-awaited sequel, *The Oregon Trail II*, had been released the prior week to great fanfare. Thus, his tantrum.

Glory locked herself in her bedroom, humming to drown out her grandmother's ministrations and her uncle's berserk proclamations. She changed into her class of '99 sweatshirt, the one with all the students' signatures on the back, and searched her desk drawers for AA batteries to resurrect her Walkman. She found them, inserted them and her Boyz II Men tape, and listened to side A, side B, and side A again before she fell asleep with her face sandwiched between pillows. She slept through her grandmother's ultimately fruitful attempts to put Uncle Keith to bed, through the many phone calls her grandmother made to all the Texas relatives, a couple church elders, her manager at the Eckerd, and the only girl she could stand on Glory's guest list — a girl named Jill whose mother said no, her daughter couldn't come. But many of Glory's relatives could, even the ones who had to be reminded whose kid Glory was. Glory slept through her grandmother's decorating schemes, cake baking and balloon inflating. She dreamt that Nate from Boyz II Men was painting her portrait on the roof of a building in some place that was definitely not China Spring, Texas — lots of ivy, a pergola, summer-weight fabrics blowing in the wind — and when she woke up she was fourteen.

In seventh grade, Derrick Naylor — the same Derrick Naylor now laid low by chlamydia — having taken the Shakespeare portion of their English course more to heart than his classmates, had called Glory an onion-eyed strumpet in front of everyone for no good reason at all. The whole lunchroom went silent, everyone stared at her as if trying to judge whether it was true. Though she was neither a tearful girl, nor any less chaste than your average seventh-grader — it had nothing to do with Glory — the insult stuck. For a moment, a month or two, she became a kind of ad hoc mascot: not *an* onion-eyed strumpet, but *the* onion-eyed strumpet.

For everyone but Glory, the insult barely survived Thanksgiving break. By December, it was forgotten. And soon enough, she was ignored again as completely as she'd ever been, save by the four girls she considered friends and the three who considered her worthy of their constant, albeit oblique, torment. The insult passed, but Glory didn't forget a thing. The second semester of her seventh-grade year was marked by a different and far more interesting calamity.

Junie's house did not look like a face no matter what angle you viewed it from—or if it did, it was a cubist face, all the animating features piled on one side. The front door opened to the laundry room and a tiny foyer where muddy boots and umbrellas were abandoned. Four brass hooks—three for coats, one for keys. Then, in order: linoleum kitchen, amber-lit living room, oakish dining room, and a long hall off which the three bedrooms were positioned. Glory's was the last stop on the line. On her door was taped a drawing dashed off by a caricaturist at Six Flags—dishwater Glory, freckles embellished to asterisks, macrocephalic, and threatening to tip the basket of the hot air balloon she was waving from—above which rainbowed, or frowned, yellow construction-paper letters spelling Glory's first and middle name, which was Rebecca. Only her grandmother called her Gloribelle. And sometimes Uncle Keith, but only when he was feeling lively.

It wasn't even noon yet when Glory woke to tires gnashing gravel in the driveway and peeked out her blinds. A minivan deposited a little boy and his mother, whom she recognized from church—an over-expressive choir singer with a rosacea blotch on her cheek the shape of a Baltic country. The boy carried a gift-wrapped box, tromping across the gravel in cowboy boots a couple sizes too big. The minivan drove away and passed another minivan. Horn toots were exchanged. The second vehicle let out Mrs. McAlister, a tiny old lady in a lavender jogging suit, and her son, Willard, who had both Down syndrome and a fixed outfit—a striped polo shirt tucked neatly into khaki shorts, a braided brown belt, socks and sandals. Willard was somewhere in his forties. He kept his doe eyes trained always on whatever middle distance was available, and, now, he shook hands rather formally with the boy in boots. The two mothers exchanged a quick hug while Mr. McAlister parked the van and joined them.

There were other cars too, parked in the grass beside Junie's Buick and Keith's pickup—trucks and vans, a bedraggled red sports car. A station wagon sat beneath a winter-bare live oak, a dozen stickers cluttering its bumper. The only one Glory could read from her window stated: "If It Ain't King James It Ain't Bible." It was a popular slogan among a certain type of people. That missing article had always annoyed Glory.

Now that she removed her headphones, she could hear the whole house abuzz with that kind of approximation to a party churchgoers call fellowship. It was ten in the morning, and whoever these people were, they were fellowshipping all over her home, in the dining room, the bathroom, marking Glory's territory with short spurts of laughter or an anecdote. She heard the word *chlamydia* used as an interjection, heard rapid sockfeet pattering down the hallway, followed by a small body's hard collision with her bedroom door. The boy in the boots, no doubt, had removed his boots and, suddenly disencumbered, gone a little wild. When he started crying, Glory heard the mother gasp. "Oh, pumpkin," the woman said. Glory made sure her door was locked, put her headphones back on, and switched the tape to side B.

It didn't take second sight to track her grandmother's nighttime machinations. Junie was never so transparent as when she was trying to bring a secret to blossom. When she tried to explain herself, that's when she became opaque.

Only the particle-board door stood between Glory and her birthday party, not the party she wanted. What she wanted rarely figured in. She could populate the party without hearing anymore of it. A few old women from church, a deacon or two, maybe an elder, uncles and aunts and their gloomy or unpacifiable children—a bunch of people she didn't care about who called her young lady, who called one another brother and sister. There would be colorful bunting and a cake with her name on it. Presents too—picture-framed verses from the Book of Proverbs or Psalms, Christian young adult novels with a secular pulse belying the beating heart a of hokey moral. It was only a matter of time before her grandmother knocked on her door and tried to cajole her out. But Glory would not be cajoled.

She had to pee, but, if it came to it, she would pee in the trashcan or sneak out her window and do it in the woods.

When the knock did come, she felt it like a tremor beneath her music, an offbeat bassline.

"Glory," her grandmother called through the door, "there's some people that want to sing happy birthday to you."

Years before, when Glory was in grade school and her birthday guests would consist of only her uncle and grandmother, the whole day would be about Glory. Uncle Keith, with the clunky black camcorder perched like a microwave on his shoulder, would film Glory dancing with her dolls, singing Reba McEntire songs into her pink karaoke microphone, garbling the lyrics, making the lyrics better. This was back before Junie's arthritis forced her to give up piano playing. They would all three share the piano bench while Junie played the happy birthday song, adorning the chords with florid doodles. All three of them sang the song, not so much in harmony, but always converging in unison on Glory's name.

And that's how it went from birthday three or four until birthday ten. Nobody had told Glory that the birthday girl wasn't supposed to sing along, not until her eleventh, when, under a crepe paper canopy, at a long table covered in a purple oilcloth, Glory, her skinny little-girl legs weighted by roller skates, had sung along with the other girls. Happy birthday to her own self. First, one girl stopped singing, followed successively by another girl, and another. Only Glory, her grandmother, and a couple chaperoning parents carried the tune across the finish line. The first girl—Heather Tabor, whom Glory hadn't spoken to since— tugged her mother's sleeve and said, "Glory's singing her own happy birthday song." Heather's mother, bless her heart, tried to teach her daughter a micro-lesson on the spot using only her eyes, about charity, about how girls without actual mommies have it hard, but the lesson didn't take. The other girls agreed with Heather. For reasons they didn't bother to, or couldn't, articulate, the birthday girl singing along to her own song was the gravest breach of etiquette. Glory spent the remainder of the last hour at the skating rink skating in circles by herself, not crying at all, determined already to be harder than hardship—this one, all future ones, and public ones especially. These kinds of things happen to ten year olds, you'd think, so they can forget them, so they can learn about the power of forgetfulness. But Glory didn't forget things like other people did.

That was before Uncle Keith lost his job and his marbles. He'd driven her home from the skating rink, kept up a nervous, cheerful chatter, and insisted that they hit the Dairy Queen drive-thru even though they'd already had cake and ice cream. Somehow Keith had understood that Glory blamed nobody for her ruined party but Junie.

He told her, "Mom loves you more than anybody. She's tried to do right by you."

Glory rolled the window down. "She's not my mom."

"I know that," Keith said. And as if he was trying to finger-plug a fresh hole in a leaky dike, he added, "Your mom should've come."

"But she can't be around me, can she? I make her sick."

Keith pushed the truck's cigarette lighter in. When it popped out, he lit his cigarette and said, "It's more complicated than that, honey. You know it is."

"Tell me," Glory said. "I'm ten. I'm old enough to know."

"Not my story to tell, girlie. I'm sorry."

Keith turned up the radio then, and that was the end of more than the conversation.

Now, Glory went to switch the Boyz II Men tape, and the tape got caught. It unspooled its guts when she tugged on it. Until she wound it back in and got it playing again, she was unfortified. Her grandmother was still at the door.

"Gloribelle," her grandmother said, "if you don't answer me, I'm gonna have to assume you're dead. And then Uncle Keith's gonna have to kick the door in. Are you dead?"

"Yes."

"Don't you want to come out and have some cake? There's a lot of people here to see you."

"No."

Junie said, "No what?"

In that instant, her grandmother's tone sharpened. A child may be petulant or mean or genuinely grieved, but none of those moods should ever preclude basic politeness. Not in her house.

"No, ma'am," Glory said.

The whole confusion surrounding Glory's provenance had been Junie's fault. It had something to do with the way the woman ordered events — not chronologically or by rank, but positioned along some convoluted emotional highway, winding past every meltdown and triumph she'd ever had or witnessed, dotted with road signs nobody but she could read. And like in a scavenger hunt, she had to hit up each stop along the way, even if it had only glancing relevance to the ultimate destination. That was how it went when she revealed to Glory who her mother was. Or tried to. Glory didn't understand for quite some time.

She could've said, "I have two children, Keith and Quinn. You're my grandbaby, which means Quinn's your mama."

She could've, but she didn't.

How to explain the fact that she'd scrubbed the house of all evidence of Quinn's existence? How to justify the fact that Quinn's name hadn't been uttered even once in Glory's presence for the first ten years of her life? And even answering those questions, however painful, would've done nothing to explain why Glory had never laid eyes on her own mother, though the woman was alive and well, living in Amarillo where she managed a Radio Shack and lived in sin with a man twenty-some-odd years her senior.

How to explain how Glory's presence had caused Quinn to become violently ill? Fever, vomiting—nerves the doctors had called it at first. Postpartum something, pathological something else. They would've called it hysteria fifty years before, or a woman's ailment fifty years before that. They hadn't been able to see the truth, because the truth contradicted science. Junie knew, though, that a complex chain of sin and punishment, righteousness and reward, had suddenly coiled itself around her household. If Quinn was allergic to her own baby girl, it was because God had ordained it from the beginning of time. Punishment for her daughter had been for Junie a miracle.

She'd wanted to tell the truth the whole time. The necessity of sustaining the lie (a sin of omission, she told herself, not commission), it swarmed her privacy like hornets. On each of Glory's birthdays, she redoubled her resolve to tell the truth, but resolve alone accomplished nothing.

The truth was that she liked having a little girl all to herself— this time without the interference of her husband, Claude, who'd gone to be with the Lord when Keith and Quinn were teenagers—a perfect little person to dress and feed and teach about the dangers of the world. A little head in her lap as they watched TV in the evenings. Hair to brush, songs to sing that didn't seem so foolish anymore when she was teaching them to a child. An opportunity, too, to do right what she'd evidently done so wrong with Quinn.

Instead of telling everything, she'd told next to nothing. She'd told Glory that God closed doors and opened windows. After all, it was right there in her name: Glory. All things work together for the glory of God, she'd said, even if they might seem confusing at the moment.

It took the fiasco of Glory's tenth birthday for the truth to come out, although not quite all at once. Glory let her grandmother coax her to the couch that evening, let her hair be brushed. Junie attributed her silence to exhaustion, the numb wave of relative peace that follows on the heels of hysteria. But Glory was sharpening her knives.

"Mama Junie?" she asked.

"What is it, honey?"

"I learned something about a girl at school," she said. "Her name's Cara, and her parents are white but she's Asian. You know why?"

Glory felt the hairbrush stall midstroke. She waited until she could feel her grandmother concocting an answer, just long enough, before she continued.

"She's adopted," Glory said. "We learned all about it in class."

One more pause now, waiting for her grandmother's intake of breath, which she would interrupt. When it came, she said:

"I wish I was adopted."

Then it came out, most of it, more or less intact, more or less accurate, through a scrim of pleas for Glory to please understand, that it was more complicated than true or false. Glory understood. What her grandmother wanted, though, had less to do with understanding than with forgiveness. If Glory had been asked the right question, she would've flat out refused.

That was before Glory began to grasp the seriousness of her power — that her capacity for destruction was not bound by time or distance, that it could be aimed and fired, and if she could learn how to do that, there would be nothing to stand between her and whatever she wanted.

Heather Tabor, the girl who'd criticized Glory's birthday

etiquette, had begun seventh grade in the same lucky echelon in which she'd ended sixth. Taller than other girls, pristine and pale, black hair like the void pulled back in a ponytail, she was slender, too, and elegant, the kind of girl who dated high school boys with her parent's permission, because wasn't she so mature for her age? So mature, in fact, that she didn't partake in the Shakespearean name-calling that fall. Glory and Glory's ilk were beneath more than Heather's contempt—they scarcely registered as coevals.

On one of these dates with one of these high school boys, they had been cruising up and down Valley Mills Drive with the other bored teenagers, showing off their parents' cars and their ability to smoke cigarettes with impunity. Their car was t-boned by a maniac driver. The boy was fine, but Heather had to wait half an hour before she could be removed from the wreckage. Her left leg had been pinioned between ragged metal and ragged metal. The paramedics couldn't do a thing. They had to bring in the serious professionals, a specialist in safety goggles who sawed her left leg off at the shin.

Heather appeared again at school only once, for half a day. Everyone applauded as the principal wheeled her into first-period geometry. Glory looked for her at lunch, not to speak to her or condole; she wanted to see how awkwardly Heather moved in her wheelchair, to scour her face for some link connecting her hatred to Heather. But after first period, she never saw Heather again.

It was difficult to pinpoint the exact moment Glory became aware of the scope of her powers—she was still grasping it—but it had to have been after Derrick Naylor's venereal ailment became public knowledge. His chlamydia formed the missing vertex of the triangle—it only became clear that it was a triangle once the new vertex appeared, a triangle for now—and only then was Glory able to get her bearings. Derrick provided the third point by which she could begin to triangulate.

There was Heather and Derrick, but the first angle of the

triangle had been Quinn, Glory's mother. The one that made the least sense. How could she have made her mother ill before she was aware of her mother, before she had time to make a memory of her face?

Glory couldn't help but wonder: if she honed her abilities would she one day be able to wield them like a sorceress would? Point her fingers, arch her knuckles, and shoot destruction from her fingertips? The way she could tune her eyes to see latent death in the people around her, it seemed so easy to find the breech in a person's protective covering, to take death like a thread and pull until the skin unraveled just enough to let her in.

But then, of course, a simpler question remained: why Derrick and not others? There were plenty of people she hated far more than Derrick. Would their time come too?

For the first time in her life, she swooned in the face of the monstrosity of time. If her powers could affect circumstances before her consciousness could apprehend them, did that not mean that they acted outside of her own will? What other way was there to explain the way she'd made her mother sick? She had protected herself on all sides, after the fact and before. Time was no limitation. Quite the opposite. It only remained for her to discover how to use what was already hers.

The day was pushing into the afternoon, and still new guests arrived. The later the guest, it seemed to Glory, the obscurer her recollection of them. The obscurer, too, their rung-position on even the most accommodating social ladder. Some of these latecomers looked like the kind of people you find in Walmart in the middle of the night, hill people wandering the cosmetics aisles with an oleaginous gleam in their eyes, part rapture, part befuddlement. Glory assumed they were relatives. Junie knocked just once more and, receiving no answer, left without a word.

As busy as Glory's room was, she found herself hopelessly bored when confined to it. Her urge to pee had passed and returned. She'd dressed and redressed, considered joining the party just to get a piece of cake, but thought better of it. All the Boyz II Men songs were blurring together now into something sticky and unlaundered, immaculate white bed sheets gone beige with sweat.

She wandered the perimeter of her room, looking at the posters and photo collages on her wall, willing them to defamiliarize before her eyes. She'd done it before. It was becoming easier. And like how looking at someone's face upside down brings all the hidden asymmetries to the surface, so she saw her friends and idols as strangers, agglomerations of bones and gooey organs covered with skin, the same way a bandage covers a wound or a garbage can covers garbage. Her smiling or clowning classmates became vehicles of decay — walking, jumping, giggling putrefaction. Shania Twain on the poster, in glittery pants and a shirt baring her midriff, standing on a hill overlooking a lake — nothing but a shiny, costumed envelope concealing purple-gray tubes transporting excrement, purple liver, purple kidney, carrion heart. If Shania Twain was grotesque, Kenny Chesney was nauseating, the brim of his hat pulled low to keep crows from pecking out his eyes. She could smell Garth Brooks rotting without even looking at his poster. She refused to look at the Boyz II Men one.

When she stood before the mirror, her image did not undergo the same morbid transformation. She was real and alive, vibrant. Her own physical imperfections and asymmetries that she'd long memorized — they were superficial. There was no way to associate the gaps between her teeth or her mismatched nostrils with death.

She cleared the mess from her desk and opened her English notebook to the first blank page. The bedroom was overheated, stuffy, but the pencil trembled in her fingers and her spine felt trimmed with bright frost. She scratched out her first sentence three times before she wrote: *Everybody that crosses me gets destroyed*. The sentence that followed began to expand upon the first when another knock sounded, muffled by her music but distinct. She pulled her headphones off and waited for it to repeat.

The knock knocked again and she realized it came from her window. She pulled the blinds back, thinking that it must be her grandmother grasping at new tactics. It wasn't. It was Uncle Keith, standing in the flowerbed with a soupy grin on his face and a clumsy shave.

Glory flipped the latches on the window and raised it.

"Happy birthday, kiddo," he said. "Let's get the heck out of here."

Keith dislodged the screen while Glory put her boots on. He gripped her by her underarms and swung her out the window.

"You wanna learn to drive?" he asked.

She didn't know what to say but yes. Anything, please, but this.

Uncle Keith let Glory out to pee at the entrance to a farm road off the highway. The passenger door only opened from the outside. He told her to hold tight and lumbered around the truck. His pivot was all wonky on the left side—a limp, but weirder; some hard-to-master move in a two-step, repeated without any music for context. A limp like that sour look on your face you were warned would stick.

Glory peed behind a juniper tree. When she returned, Uncle Keith was in the passenger seat, smoking a cigarette with the window down.

He said, "Sink or swim's my motto."

If she sat on the edge of the seat, the seat belt stretched tight across her chest, she could just reach the pedals. If her grandmother knew what she was doing, she'd scream. Or faint, or die.

The road was empty, rolling past clusters of mailboxes, February trees, and little else. Uncle Keith didn't say anything when the tires veered into roadside gravel. He didn't chastise her or change his posture at all. Only once did he put his huge hairy hand on the wheel, just to keep it steady as they passed the only car they'd pass at all.

Keith smoked one cigarette after another and sipped at a can of Dr. Pepper. His shirt buttons strained against his belly. There was a little gray at his temples that Glory hadn't ever noticed. She watched him in her periphery, waiting for him to do something or say something, but he seemed content to play silent passenger.

"Who all was at the house?" she asked when the silence started weighing.

"Oh, church people, some cousins" Keith said. "Good to be out of there."

"I thought you liked church people."

"They're all right on Sunday," he said, "when you've been prepping all week to see them. Better than cousins."

"Was my mom there?"

"Go ahead and turn left at the T," he said. "Put your blinker on. Ease up on the gas."

He dropped his cigarette into his Dr. Pepper can and threw the can into the truck bed.

"Good job, girlie," he said. "Not too fast, not too slow." He wedged his thumbs behind his belt buckle and eased it off his belly. "Don't you think if your mama was there we'd have told you?"

"Nobody tells me anything."

"It's your birthday," Keith said. "What do you wanna know?"

Glory adjusted her behind against the seat. She didn't know her uncle well enough anymore to decide if he was laying a trap.

"You won't tell her?"

"Who, your grandma? I'm no tattletale."

She made him promise, and he did. And he made her slow the truck down before the turnoff to Delmar Ranch Road. It wasn't much of a road, though—just muddy wheel ruts between which buff grass grew bent. Another sign, spray-painted with an inverted silver swastika, said *No River Access*, which meant that there was.

"Final lesson," he said. "Reverse means everything's inside

out. You gotta do it over your shoulder."

Keith directed her as she turned the truck around and lined up the back window with the foreshortening road. He told her to go slower when she went backward. The brain, he said, isn't too good at wrapping itself around counterintuitive stuff, so you have to proceed with caution. She wondered if Keith had planned this out—no traffic, the straightest roads. Driving wasn't such a big deal. When the river bluffs came into view, he declared her a natural.

"You don't tell your grandma I let you drive," he said, "and I won't tell her you was asking questions. Deal?"

"Deal."

"Three seem like a fair number?"

She told him three was perfect.

He dragged an ice chest to the rocky embankment overlooking the Bosque River. It was full of Dr. Pepper and ice, two slices of purloined birthday cake wrapped to paper plates with plastic. He'd forgotten to bring forks. They sat on the ground and ate with their hands. All the while, Glory concocted her questions—she thought she knew which three, but ordering them was crucial.

Beneath their perch, the river ran thinly leftward, whichever cardinal direction that was.

Uncle Keith took his shoes off and dangled his sockfeet over the rock ledge. He suppressed a belch and asked her what she was waiting for. "Ask away," he said.

"Fine." The sky overhead was marshy and streaked with filigrees of sunlight. Glory wanted there to be some ceremony preparatory to her questions, but she didn't know what kind. "Do I really make her sick?" she asked. "Because that sounds fake."

"Oh boy, I was hoping for where do babies come from."

"You said you'd answer."

"I did," he said. He rummaged for something to do with his hands. "She's a weird one, your mom. And she was real sick. I thought she was faking at first, but she wasn't. I can't say whether it was you that did it."

"Just say it," Glory said.

"Maybe she was allergic to Mom," Uncle Keith said. "That would make more sense."

"People aren't allergic to other people," Glory said. "Say it."

"Honey, I don't know what you want me to say. I don't have a better answer than that."

"You do," Glory said. "You were there. All I got is your story and her story, and y'all aren't telling it all. You know a hundred percent more than I do."

"That's the best I can do, Gloribelle," Uncle Keith said. "You got two more questions."

"Fine," Glory said. Now that she understood her uncle was indeed playing a trick on her, she had to discard and reassemble her remaining questions on the fly. "How do you know if you're good at something?" she asked. "Like really good at it."

"Well," he said. He reclined on an elbow and seemed to ponder. Clusters of water bugs skated in quick bursts across the surface of the river, not pausing long enough to do anything, but pausing nonetheless. Glory couldn't see them, but she could see the ripples they left behind. "I suppose some people are just good at things without even trying. And then there's the rest of us who gotta keep failing over and over before we even get an idea what it would look like to succeed."

Glory stopped listening when he began to move from the general to the particular. Now he was only talking about himself, his own inability to discern what the world had set in front of him. He would soon be wading through clichés — ninety-nine percent perspiration, stick-to-itiveness. Glory buried her hands in the cavity between her crossed knees and her crotch. She gripped her right pinky finger in her left fist, bent it back against the sharpness of not so much pain as the needle-bright pressure of connectivity, the dizzying sensation that the kneebone is indeed connected to the thigh bone, the anus to the mouth, the heart to the brain.

The sensation shot up from the pulse point in her wrist, through the center of her forearm, through her bicep, and into her chest. She imagined herself possessed of the ability to manipulate both hands this way. A symmetry of, again, not pain — of whatever this sensation was, pain for lack of a better word — and the two pains meeting at her solar plexus, commingling, and some sort of transaction being accomplished. She had no idea what kind, or what would be the result, but for a moment she wanted only that.

She interrupted her uncle.

"I still got a third question," she said, "and it's hard to explain. It's not even really a question."

"I'm nothing but ears."

If Glory thought too hard about it, there were too many things to say and no perfect order to say them in. It felt like juggling — how do you begin? She wrenched her finger further back, and threw her thoughts up in the air at once.

"Okay, so, I guess I'm afraid that I can't control what I do to people," she said, "and what I do to people is what I'm good at. The only thing I'm good at. Like with my mom."

"I don't follow."

"Hold on," she said. "I told you it's hard to say."

Keith bowed his head, and Glory continued:

"First, my mom. She wasn't gonna be a good mom, so I stopped her from being one. By making her sick. And then this girl got her leg amputated because I hated her. Next, it was a boy I wasn't even mad at anymore, even though he said nasty things. He's on his deathbed. And next it's you."

"Me?"

Glory kept her eyes trained on the river, following the waterbugs' erratic movement until it didn't seem so erratic, until a pattern emerged, like how a smattering of stars becomes a constellation once you connect the dots.

"Yeah," she said, "and I don't want to hurt you. But, it's like, I don't think I can help it. I asked you to tell me the truth and you won't."

He said, "Glory, I don't know what more I can tell you."

"And Grandma Junie says we gotta take care of you."

He turned his body to face her, but she stayed fixed on the waterbugs.

"Honey, I don't need taking care of," he said. "Y'all don't gotta worry about me."

"She says it's like the McAlisters at church with their boy." She was saving eye contact for when it would be most effective, punctuation so bold it would gouge the page. "They had him and they love him, but they gotta take care of him for the rest of their lives. And when—"

Keith said, "Willard McAlister is a handicapped boy."

"He's not a boy, though. He's as old as you are. And they're not much older than Grandma Junie. What's gonna happen when they die? Who's gonna take care of him?"

Keith pulled his feet up from the edge of the bluff and dragged one leg across the other.

"She made me promise that when she dies I'll always take care of you. And I want to. I know I should, but I'm scared I'm gonna hurt you."

"She said that?" he asked. "That you're supposed to take care of me?"

Glory let her finger go, and it sprung back to rejoin the others. "She didn't want me tell you," she said. She let her eyes find his. "But if y'all can't tell the truth, I'm going to.

Keith pinched the bridge of his nose. When he finally stood, even over the musty river stench, Glory could smell death seeping from his pores.

When they got back to the house, the sun had already gone most of the way down and there wasn't a car but Junie's in the driveway. She must've heard them approaching, because she was standing by the San Pedro cactus with her arms crossed and a look of tired bewilderment on her face. Her party clothes, whatever they'd been, had been replaced by pajama pants dappled with bleach stains and a giant yellow sweatshirt. Keith barely waited for Glory to climb out of the truck before he threw it in reverse.

"Where's he going?" Junie called. "What are you doing, Keith?"

Without hitch or hiccup, Glory said, "I think he's having an episode. He was talking about some crazy stuff."

"Oh," said Junie. "Are you okay?"

"Yeah, I'm fine. I feel bad for him."

Junie took her by the shoulders and appraised her. "Are you sure you're okay?"

"I'm great," Glory said. "Uncle Keith just wants to be alone."

"Oh," Junie said, "okay." For a moment, she seemed to flounder, like a woman who'd mislaid her keys. Without makeup, the bruisy bags beneath her eyes were tinged the same yellow as her shirt. She blinked and seemed to regain what passed for her as composure, a stiffening of the spine, a recollection of what she'd been mad about a moment before. "It was awful rude of you to abandon your guests."

"They were your guests," Glory said. "Let's go in."

"Are you hungry?" Junie asked. "There's all kinds of food. You got a whole pile of gifts in there too."

"What did you get me?"

"It's in the pile," Junie said. "It's a surprise. You gotta open it."

Junie kicked her slippers off inside the front door. Glory kept her boots on. Stacks of chocolate-stained, red party plates crowded around the sink, which itself was full of red party cups. Boxes of fried chicken from Grandy's were piled by the trashcan. Over the mantle frowned, or rainbowed, a happy birthday banner.

"It's pretty messy in here," Glory said.

"Well, I was hoping Keith would help me straighten up."

Glory said, "You know what I want for my birthday more

than anything?"

"What, dear?"

"The birthday song. But I guess it's too late now."

"Good Lord, honey. We'd have sang it for you if you'd have shown yourself."

"Me and Uncle Keith were at the river," Glory said. "I want you to sing it."

"You're being strange, Glory," Junie said. She couldn't decide where to stand or sit, so she hovered, poked at the dirty dishes, gave up. She was tired. "You should eat something."

"Not hungry," Glory said. "Sing the song."

"Fair enough," Junie said. "It is your birthday. You know I can't carry a tune to save my life."

"And play it," Glory said. "On the piano."

"Honey, my hands are—"

"Your hands are fine," Glory said. "Play."

Junie pulled the piano bench out and sat heavily. She pulled her sleeves back. It had been years since she'd played anything, but her fingers fit against the keys so smoothly. She pressed a middle C. Her hands did feel fine.

"You wanna sing with me, Glory? It's embarrassing to sing all by myself."

"You start," Glory said, "and I'll join in."

Glory sat behind her grandmother in the leather recliner. She pulled the lever that made it recline. Above the smell of fried chicken, she could smell the breath and body odor of all the birthday guests lingering in the carpet and couch cushions, hanging in the air light as cirrus clouds, beneath which hung her grandmother's personal odor.

Junie pressed a D into the keys and followed it with a little flourish.

"All right, Glory. Here goes."

Junie's voice was agile for a woman her age, for a woman who sang so infrequently. It only took a couple notes for her to remember why she loved singing. An audience wasn't necessary.

The triangle had become a square, and Glory foresaw that shape's further expansion. New points meant more surface area, more space in which Glory's power could expand. Against the arms of the recliner, she bent her pinkies back until they nearly touched their own metacarpals — the surge from her left hand met the surge from her right, behind her heart, and there it articulated a many-sided, undulating shape, which she knew had always been there, and which, like the image hidden in the neon furrows of a Magic Eye picture, once she saw could never again unsee.

"Come on, Gloribelle," Junie said. "Sing with me. You only turn fourteen once."

Glory raised her fingers at her grandmother, arched her knuckles. She didn't know what to do next. What colors would destruction be when it poured from her fingertips? She didn't know, but she was prepared to wait until she was shown.

SONNET FOR SISYPHUS

what the story fails to tell us is the gods/
gave sisyphus/ a little more weight
than he could bear/what the story fails
to tell us/ is eventually sisyphus will
run out of breath/ that his arms will
lose strength/that his legs will grow
heavy/ that the rock will feel heavy/
too heavy/ to push/ anymore/ that
sisyphus will fall/that the rock will crush
his frail body/that as he sees the rock/
about to crush/his frail body/ he will
think to himself/ i wonder if the gods are
watching me/ i wonder if they remember
me/ i wonder if they remember me.

ARS POETICA SONNET #3

Maybe the sonnet is not like Terrance Hayes
said a little room in a house set aflame but
rather/ a ring/ in which the boxer must fight
against himself/ in which all his ideas fight
for control/ fight/ not to be cornered/ maybe
the sonnet is the prayer/ the boxer says before
the match/ overflowing with fear/ maybe
it's the mouth guard/ always on the verge
of breaking/ maybe it's the sweat/that spills
onto the floor/ nothing/ but a product of
the body/ maybe it's a series of soft jabs/
preceding/ a knockout punch / maybe it's
the hope of a knockout punch/ a knockout
punch/ that sometimes never comes.

THE QUESTION OF WHERE

It was the winter after your death,
darkness coming early, a shadow
that lingered until late morning,
my days spent gazing out the window,
my mind never leaving the question
of where. You had been so present,
how could you be gone, and to where —
to out beyond the hills, over the lakes
of our summers, beneath the soil
of your gardening days? Where, where,
my brain tugged the question from
morning till evening. My hands found
work in the mixing, stirring, pushing,
pulling of breadmaking, a new pursuit
that filled the long hours, the rhythm
of rising and resting and rising again
a song that sang me through winter days
until light waxed us into spring, earth
greened and the where of my searching
quieted into the steady beat of my heart.

EVEN TODAY

Language does the best it can.
— Linda Pastan

Even today, sky mute as our aging dog,
I search for words — the *abc*'s of a childhood
when books were a late day treat, when lamplight
softened the room where my coal-mining father —
later, my uranium-enrichment-plant-
working father — and my stay-at-home mother
sat with their open books, pages turning
like the flutter of leaves against the window,
my sisters and I sprawled on the floor, *Childcraft*
volumes open to nursery rhymes or fairytales —
the gingham dog and the calico cat forever
battling while the owl and the pussycat put out
to sea, and Rapunzel lowered her golden
tresses, and language crept upon us, quiet
as the dishes out in the kitchen, the last
vestiges of water drying on their shiny
surfaces where an hour earlier we had
propped them in the rack, each caress of a hand
a benediction on a day's work, the long
evening calling us, and though wordless,
our young selves turned toward language the way
the sun daily turned from ridge to zenith,
and slipped once more into the hollow where
all we loved breathed our same air.

There was no one else outside except the birds.

WHAT SHE FOUND THERE

Amy found the ring at CVS in the school supply aisle between pencils and Post-it notes. She tried to buy it, but the ring said not for sale, and the frat boy looking clerk confirmed: It's on the house, probably thinking she was crazy for wanting such an ugly throw-away thing. Of course, she didn't know what it was, that it was special. Instead, it looked more like a gumball machine ring or some lame toy that was a favor in a Chuck E. Cheese goodie bag. But nonetheless the ring appealed to her. In a way it spoke to her, as if to say in some Gollum *Lord of the Rings* voice but less creepy: *You have to have me.*

She was looking for thumb tacks with which to pin up reminders to Jason on the corkboard he kept at the place he was staying. She wasn't posting reminders for things like "take out the trash" or "wash the dishes." He was good at those things. Instead, the reminders were for the more essential things: "Remember that your name is Jason." "You live at 1421 Elm Avenue." "Your sister's name is Marjorie." "You are 42 years old." That last reminder she was about to strike out and change to 43. His birthday was in three weeks.

She didn't like to use technical terms for his condition, instead she just thought of it as him losing himself in bits and pieces.

Amy wasn't sure why she picked up the ring and put it on even though it looked like it was made of plastic. At least that first night it did. But she knew why she kept it on her hand.

After she took three buses to get to Jason, he looked at the ring and smiled. "There it is," he said pointing to the ring. "I'm so glad you've found it.

She didn't argue with him or tell him that she'd never seen it before and neither had he. Instead, she just told him: "I'm glad too" because, for the moment, she was.

She stayed with him an hour, then took the same three buses back home. The bus stop wasn't particularly convenient. It was at the bottom of a steep hill on a road without a sidewalk, and she had to walk up it while dodging cars, bikers, and mopeds to get to her small two bedroom apartment.

"More like a bedroom and a closet," her mother had said on the day she'd first seen it. And the pride that she'd felt at picking something on her own and paying for it was gone. All the pretty frills seemed frayed around the edges when she viewed them through her mother's eyes.

Amy had been excited to show her the refrigerator with the built-in ice maker. Her mother didn't even have one of those. Her mother had pointed out that the ice had a weird aftertaste. And then Amy noticed it too.

Amy heated up a frozen pizza in a green package. It was $5 but touted itself as healthy. The wheat pizza crust kind of tasted like cardboard.

Amy liked cooking in the oven though. She felt like the oven food was fresher, crisper, more real. Plus, the microwave smelled of Peter's curry, which he had made five years ago. No matter what she'd done, she couldn't get the smell out of the microwave or the stain off her cabinet. "You like Indian, right?" he had said after he'd already began making it. And she could see that the only acceptable answer was yes, so she had nodded. And he had continued staining her counter and making her microwave smell of a foreign land that she had never traveled to and never would.

Amy had never been outside of Ohio.

Sometimes, Amy had dreams of kissing Peter, and she woke up in a cold sweat both frustrated and relieved. Frustrated that she still had these dreams and relieved that he wasn't here, that he never would be again.

When she met Jason, Amy thought her life had finally changed for the better.

After Jason complimented the ring, Amy noticed that the ring looked fresher, brighter, newer. It looked as good, she thought, as all the costume jewelry she owned, even the gold plated stuff with cubic zirconia.

She would wear it tomorrow to work, she decided. She fell asleep feeling satisfied, or almost satisfied, something she hadn't felt in a long time.

Amy was never ready to wake up when her alarm rang at 5 a.m. But she had to be at work at 7, and it was an hour commute to the paper factory. Amy didn't have a car, but she had a friend, Jolene, who picked her up every morning in her blue truck. The condition was that Amy had to be ready and waiting outside, even when it was only 12 degrees out.

"Don't make me late, okay?" Jolene had said when she'd suggested the arrangement. Amy was overjoyed about the offer, even if it meant standing outside in the cold. At least it meant that she wouldn't have to walk to the bus stop every morning risking death and dirty clothes.

"I'll be there," Amy had said, and she always was.

Jolene used the car ride to work to talk about her latest boyfriend. This week it was Joel in accounting.

"He has such big arm muscles," Jolene was saying as she shifted gears.

Amy nodded. Jolene never asked her about herself, about her love life, and Amy was glad. There was nothing much to say. Besides, Amy liked being able to vicariously participate in Jolene's adventures. She could love the men while Jolene did. This usually lasted a week or two and hate the men when Jolene began to pick them apart. That was weeks three and four. Week five or six was the break-up.

"It's nothing major," she said about Brad, the man before Joel. "He's just such a loud chewer."

Derrick's flaw had been that Jolene looked too much like his ex.

Amy had one half-hour break and two fifteen-minute breaks "if time permitted." They had to make their quotas. The break room was a windowless room that faced the river, not that Amy could see it. Not that she wanted to. It was contaminated with the chemicals that the plant spewed out.

Sometimes, Amy ate. More often, she read spy novels set in the former Soviet Union. She had loved Jack Ryan. The fall of the Soviet Union made Amy a little sad. Now, there was nothing big and concrete to fear, just a bunch of smaller things: unnamed, unknown terrorists, hidden away in countries where Amy imagined they didn't read Bibles.

After work, Amy met Jolene outside at her truck. Jolene noticed the ring the second day.

"Where'd you get that?" Jolene asked.

Amy never lied, but she had enough sense to now.

"My father gave it to me," Amy said.

"Mind if I try it on?" Jolene asked with envy in her eyes.

"I don't think it will come off."

For effect, Amy pretended to pull it.

"Here, let me try," Jolene said, grabbing her hand and yanking at the ring.

To Amy's surprise, it really wouldn't budge, even though it had gone on easily two days ago.

"Guess it must be all that fast food you eat," Jolene said.

Amy didn't eat fast food, but she agreed anyway. "Must be," Amy said.

Jolene seemed satisfied with this response and began talking about Joel again.

Peter's kisses were too forceful. That was the main reason that Amy didn't miss him, though not the only one, even though Amy's mother had referred to him as "a catch."

He looked good on paper, Amy wanted to say, but she didn't. She didn't say anything. Instead, she just listened to her mother's disappointed sigh before she tuned out the rest.

Amy had met Jason at a speech on the former Soviet Union, one that she had walked to on a whim. The speech had turned out to be dull and uninspiring. And, Amy, in disappointment, was about to walk down the road to the bus stop. Amy must have looked forlorn because Jason had seen her frown and asked, "That bad?"

"It was pretty bad," Amy said.

Jason had laughed and asked her if she wanted a drink. Amy looked to see if there was someone behind her.

Then, she finally said: "Who me?"

"I think there were only five people at this speech, and you and I were the only people under 65," he said. Amy hadn't really paid attention to the crowd. She had just stared at the speaker hoping that if she stared at him long enough and hard enough, he would become interesting.

He took her to a bar just a few miles from the lecture hall. They had talked for two hours about the former U.S.S.R. and the things that made it great and the reasons it had failed. He drove her home and didn't try to force himself in like Peter would have. Instead, he said he would call her, and he had.

They had three good months together before she realized anything was wrong. Sometimes, he would look at her and seem not to remember who she was. This after they had made love for hours.

"Tell me about what's wrong," she said to him quietly one day, one day when he still looked at her like he knew her.

And he had.

After he had dropped her off that night, Amy cried herself to sleep.

Amy hadn't told Jolene about Jason. She hadn't told her mother about him. Sometimes, she wondered if he was real. But she had a picture on her phone of him that she could take out and look at when she doubted. He was handsome and shirtless, the stubble on his face starting to grow. But this only made him more handsome. He was the kind of man who usually wouldn't have dated a girl like Amy, Amy with her Coke bottle glasses, unfashionably long dresses and shelves of books about countries that no longer existed. Her hair long and straight pulled back on the sides into a silver barrette, her face without makeup. Jason looked like the kind of man who could be a celebrity, a rustic actor who played a desperate man, more charming in his rusticness. Right now, Jason was a desperate man.

At first, Jason had had an apartment. He kept it, "in case he got better," but they both knew that he wasn't getting better. He was the kind of man who surely had been popular once.

Now, he was mostly alone, except for his sister, who, to her surprise, seemed to approve of Amy.

"Thank you for taking care of him," she told her one day after they'd both nearly collided on their visits. Amy on her way in, Marjorie on her way out.

Amy wondered if people thought that she was his caretaker. What did people think? She certainly wasn't the kind of woman who looked like she'd be with a man like that.

Lovemaking with Jason was fantastic because he was hungry, hungry to hang on to love and life. Jason was old enough to still see a 32-year-old woman as young, even though Amy was sure that people like her mother viewed her as an old maid. As if life was as simple as Jane Austen novel. She could have married Peter. Her mother thought she should have married Peter. She told Amy that the breakup was "the biggest mistake of her life."

At the home, they took good care of Jason. He almost never smelled like poop and pee even though sometimes he lost control of his bowel movements. He wore an adult diaper. When Amy had first seen that, she had gone into the bathroom and cried before she could collect herself enough to go wait for the bus.

When Amy went to see Jason again, he said: "Hey, beautiful. I see that you still have my ring."

Amy nodded. Instinctively she held out her hand, and he touched it with such tenderness that Amy wished that she was like some women who had no shame. She wished that she could at least climb into bed with him and hold him.

"What's your favorite Jack Ryan novel?" she asked him because it was a question that they had previously discussed for hours.

He preferred *The Hunt for Red October*, and she liked *Patriot Games*. He said that maybe it was a gender thing, that *Patriot Games* was a more romantic novel.

He said, "Who's Jack Ryan?" and her heart sank. "Do I know someone named Jack Ryan?"

"No," she said because it was basically the truth, and, in the end, what did we have, the books we had read or the people? "It's okay," she said, even though it wasn't.

That night, she dreamt of Jason not Peter, and it was a pleasant dream. That morning she put her fingers on the ring for the first time and wished.

"Amy," she said, when she visited him.

She couldn't remember when the last time was that he had said her name.

She asked his nurse if it would be okay if she took him outside.

The nurse said she didn't see why not. There was nothing wrong with his legs.

There was no one else outside except the birds. They had come for the feeders that the staff had installed to make the place look nice and homey. For what it was, the place was nice, but it wasn't homey. Nothing really was homey except home. She didn't think he would ever be going home.

Outside, she kissed him and kissed him, as if she never had before and if she never would again.

They kissed until their lips were chapped and it got dark and she finally had to leave in order to catch her buses.

"I love you," she said. She had never said it to him before. She didn't know if she would ever say it to him again. She didn't know if he would hear her or understand.

Clear eyed, he looked back at her, like he knew who she was. "I love you, too," he said. "When will you be back?"

For the first time in a long time, Amy thought about buying a car. It didn't have to be a nice car or a good car but a car that would take her to work so that she wouldn't have to hear Jolene's boyfriend stories and so that she could sometimes visit Jason after work, not just on the weekends.

She found an ad on the Internet and called. She rubbed the ring for luck.

Amy had $5,000 saved because she never did anything. The car cost her three. The previous owner seemed nice. She trusted him. It had been his mother's car, he explained. She had gone into a nursing home. She never had driven it anywhere but church and the grocery store. "You know what that's like," he said. She nodded. She knew all too well.

When Amy got there, that Wednesday, the first time she had driven her car anywhere, Marjorie was there. Maybe, Amy thought, Jason had other visitors during the week.

"How are you?" Majorie asked. Marjorie was one of those women with short carefully groomed hair. Trendy like Amy's mother, but nice. Amy's mother had once told her that her hair made her look like someone who had joined a cult. After that, Amy stubbornly refused to talk about it or cut it. Peter had liked it, sort of. "Women shouldn't have short hair," he said. "It's unfeminine." Peter had definite opinions about everything.

"I'm fine," Amy lied. Then she ventured a question. "His mother. Does she ever come?"

Marjorie shook her head. "She can't bear to see him like this."

"I understand," Amy said, though she didn't. Seeing him like this was better than the alternative, not seeing him at all.

Jason perked up when she saw her.

"How's my girl?" Jason asked, his tone unmistakably affectionate, and Amy colored red. She didn't know what Marjorie knew about them. If she knew, what did she think?

"I'm glad you're here," Marjorie told her. Amy felt amazement but nodded. Marjorie left. Before Amy left, she got up the courage to ask if it might be okay if she took him on a day trip. She didn't know where she planned to take him — the park, the library, to a movie about the Soviet Union or just to her apartment. She didn't know how long he had, but she wanted to be with him.

That night, before she left, he surprised her by saying, "*The Hunt for Red October* is clearly superior because it was the first. The beginning of everything."

"And beginnings," she asked, "are they always better than endings?"

The next morning, Amy planned to tell Jolene that she didn't need to ride with her anymore because she had a car. But Jolene surprised her by talking about Travis, a man she had broken up with two years ago.

"I heard that Travis was getting married," Jolene said.

"Oh yeah," Amy said.

"Yeah, and it makes me kind of sad."

"Do you feel that way with all of them or just him?"

"Sometimes," she said, "I feel like I'm too hard on them," she admitted before she began to pick Joel apart.

Amy realized that she couldn't tell her about the car that morning. Maybe she would tomorrow. Or maybe she wouldn't tell her at all.

Amy's mother called that night, and Amy let it go to voicemail. Amy wanted to visit Jason not spend half an hour wasting her time arguing about nothing.

When she got to the home, Amy got word that the visit had been approved.

On the form she filled out, Amy had to list her relationship to the patient, and Amy didn't know what to write.

"I didn't know you were engaged," the nurse said. "That ring is beautiful."

Amy didn't realize that she had put the ring on her ring finger or that it looked real.

"Congratulations," the nurse said, and Amy thanked her.

When she got to his room, she told him that she could take him home with her Saturday. "To stay?" he asked.

"Just for a visit," she admitted. "I got a car."

"What does your mother think of it?"

"She doesn't know."

"Are you going to tell her?"

"I don't know."

It took her five minutes before she realized that she was having a perfectly normal conversation with him.

"I love you," he said before she left.

"I love you, too."

"I'm glad that you like the ring," he said.

Saturday, she took him home and they made love. She didn't want to take him back. But she knew she had to.

Maybe someday, she thought but didn't have the courage to say, I can bring him home for good.

She didn't know if she could care for him or what kind of care he would need. She didn't know if his seeming recovery was temporary or if it would last for good, but she remembered their second date in which he had told her that she was the most beautiful girl he had ever seen, and she thought he was crazy.

"I'm not like most people," he said.

"I can see that," she said. She wanted to ask him what he was doing with her.

"There might come a time when you come to regret this," he said, and she wondered if he was married or a criminal. When she realized that he was only losing his mind, it had come as something of a relief.

He had seen her and he had loved her. Maybe that was enough. Still, that night, she took the ring and put her right hand over it, and she wished.

She didn't know what kind of power it had or if it had any at all. But what she did know is that she had nothing to lose.

175

LOVE POEM TO OSWALD

For me, you left your wife; you took a room
in somebody's basement and got sick.
You said you were worried, lying there,
that no one would take care of you;
that you would die unasked for. I was
repulsed by the weight of you, locking me
in like rocks. I hated your leap back
to an infant state. I hated your need for
a warm body; an Amazonian breast,
against which you could go completely limp.
Oswald, I can't help you. Last night I watched
you walk by. Your class went off in a crowd;
then, all by yourself, you brought up the rear.
You walk bravely, but you drag one leg,
as if your body were a slice of the pain you're
in, and it is. You hoped I would pick you out.
You figured it out by the stars. Always wanting
to be picked out; unforgivably passive, your
mind's a leaping fire! When I talk about you,
people say: "What's his problem?" I defend
you. You want me to defend you. I defend you
naturally. I am one of you. I defend you at once.

ON THROWING AWAY MY DAUGHTER'S CHRISTMAS CARD PHOTO

For twelve long months that picture of you
and your friends posing for a Christmas photo,
by you with careful forethought made,
has decorated my refrigerator door:
one with antlers for ears; another with
ears of elf; another with satin dress and bow,
and you in Santa's floppy hat and carpeted
boots, laughing as you leap, arms draped across
each other's shoulders, loose as Christmas holly.
I must have taken it down, along with
a few loved others, as I hurriedly cleaned
and cleared, preparing for this year's Thanksgiving
feast. And now, when you ask me for it,
lamenting that you have lost all others
in your own life's crazy shuffle, still I
cannot find it, though sorting through my
drawers among the dog-eared others, not
wanting anything I have ever loved
to be lost — old familiar cards, treasured
notes, photos dear — still I cannot find it,
this thing most deeply loved by you; amongst
the brightest jewels of your college days;
crown of your special abilities —
signifier of friends long loved, now
no longer near — oh how your disappointed
eyes, sick of my tutelage in selfishness,
rebuke me harshly then!

LONGFELLOW HOUSE / WASHINGTON'S HEADQUARTERS

Heavy curtains caught the war maps flying
and a fistful of man-tablets
may have made the battles fiercer,
but for two cannons dropped along the way
off a crumbling bridge somewhere connecting
Ticonderoga to the rest of what was then America,
ready for a fight.
And powdered mothers packing blunderbusses
might have sparked their fragrant shouts
with less bitterness had the drapes been drawn,
somebody ready at the rolling pin
and the currants sweetened with berries
children gathered in the moments before bedtime.

JULY 7

The flight of birds is the easiest event to print
black checks on a light background
*V*s vibrating their way across the sky.

A seed spit in the tree house corner
some smudge left in a stairwell
marks our passage.

And though we revere the singularity of a fingerprint
it's the random fall of the white mulberry,
a *ping* when it hits the pot,
that calls us to our ears
that opens that twosome to the sound of a new month

dog shuffle down in the jewel weed
new leaves giving way.

"Oh, yes," the secretary liked to recall, "you're the one who brought the magazines in the Jack Daniels box."

OZYMANDIAS

At that point in the morning when the tropical heat begins to ooze through the jacaranda trees and the sky tries to decide what it's going to do, my doorbell rings. It's this burly, jovial guy with a wide, friendly face.

"Good morning, boss." He smiles.

Rarely does someone ring my bell. By the way he starts with the small talk — what nice shade trees, etc. — I sense that he's going to ask for something. And when it comes to people asking for handouts, I have a firm, unwavering policy: sometimes yes and sometimes no.

When I give him a look of impatience, he goes straight to the point, "Do you have any shoes to spare?"

The request seems disarmingly intimate, not quite like asking for used toothbrushes or underwear, but almost. Yet something about its originality is appealing.

"Yes," I say at once, catching him by surprise. I search the back of my closet and return with a bag full of shoes. Six pairs. I keep only the hiking shoes I'm wearing.

The guy walks away happy. And I feel lighter, almost weightless. But there's something unsettling about this visit: he didn't seem worn down like someone who's been going from house to house, but rather as if he'd come directly to me.

I feel like an investigator piecing together the clues.

As I sit at my computer, the alarm on my watch goes off. I've had this watch forever and I've never set the alarm. But lately, inexplicably, it suddenly starts to chime. Is it some kind of reminder, and if so, a reminder of what? Does one receive warnings when one's final day has come? Like the flashing light in the cockpit in the moments before a crash?

Curious changes have been happening to my body. Wild hairs sprout from my ears while my legs look like they've been waxed. My sweat smells unfamiliar and my fingers feel overly smooth, as if my prints are disappearing. My gums are receding and my eyes have sunk into my head. I dim the light in the bathroom so I won't see my face too clearly.

When I was young, I had no patience with old people. They walked so slowly in front of you in a store. They couldn't hear you and they couldn't understand you. Now, at eighty-four, I feel the same restless uncertainty I felt when I was young. Only now, it's not about what to do with my life, but rather how it will end. I feel like an enraptured theatergoer, eager to see how things will turn out.

Finding my inbox empty, I go back through my messages and erase them one by one. What's the reason for holding onto them? A need to feel relevant? A fear of being left with none at all?

Abruptly, a message pops up on the screen. To my surprise, it's from the university. I haven't heard from them since I retired. It says they're holding a book fair and they're asking for donations.

I immediately start packing my books.

When I get angry at growing old, I look for someone to blame. Why not my neighbors? They're dropping like flies.

Like the tiny old man with the oversized bald head who lived across the street. For years I watched him grow smaller as his grandsons, twice his height but with the same large head, tinkered with their antique cars. They always had two or three parked in front, washing and shining them while the old guy observed. Sometimes his daughter, a homebody, would serve him juice, or her sons would drive him around. Then I didn't see him for days and the watchman told me he'd died. I was stunned, having believed he would always be there—shrinking, but still there.

"I'm sorry to hear that," I told the watchman. "Will his daughter and grandsons stay?"

"She's not his daughter," the watchman said. "She was his cleaning lady. He let her live there with her sons, and he left them the house."

A few houses down lived the couple I dubbed the Vaudevillians. You'd often see them parading up the street, the old woman three steps ahead, wearing a sequined dress, wrapped in a feather boa, and carrying a parasol. Lagging behind was her husband in a funereal dark suit, a black fedora, and large, clown-sized shoes. His back was so bowed from osteoporosis that he stared intently at the ground as she badgered him to keep up.

One night, awakened by a commotion, I saw him being hauled out, cadaver-like, to a noisily idling car. I was sure he was dead or dying but the next week there he was, trailing behind his wrinkled, besequinned diva, as she admonished him to keep pace. Then I didn't see him for a while and the watchman said he was dead.

"What will his wife do?" I asked.

"He wasn't her husband," the watchman said. "He used to help her run her school."

"She had a school?"

"Many years ago, but she kept him around."

And then there was the neighbor who motored around in his wheelchair, starting up conversations with anyone who passed. And the woman who coughed horrendously day and night, accompanied in a comic duet by her parrot. Death has been marching steadily up the block, going from house to house, like a messenger delivering bills.

When I was young, I clung to life as if clinging to the edge of a cliff. I did ceaseless push-ups, gobbled vitamins, slurped down raw eggs.

And I faithfully followed this cardinal rule: Never wish for time to pass: for spring to come or the rain to end, a package to arrive or an embarrassing moment to fade. A hangover to wane or a wound to heal. Every hour spent longing for time to pass is an hour that is lost.

And every hour lost brings you closer to the end.

First, I pack the books which no longer seem important. Manuals, textbooks, works once heralded as avant garde. Then come the ones that tug at my heart. Some going back to undergrad, when I haunted used bookstores like a gambler haunts the tracks. The anticipation of finding a coveted volume, the thrill when it finally appeared. The smell of the shop on a rainy afternoon, the jingle of the bell above the door. I caress an old copy of Aristotle's *Poetics* and toss it in the box with the rest.

Many conjure up memories of the phases of my life: Socrates for my classical period; Hobbes, political; Heidegger, existential. They've been at my side though relocations, divorces, and floods. I feel closer to them than to most of the people I've known. And I feel their reproach as I turn them loose. But I can't stop now. Something's been set on its course.

The alarm chimes again, with even more insistence. I quickly snap it off.

Death is something I always felt immune from. Like someone immune from poverty by virtue of an inheritance. Or someone immune from scandal by virtue of a pristine soul.

The doctor says nothing's wrong with me but he cannot be believed. How is it possible to ignore all the signs? The persistent odor of rotting meat, the wilting plants, the kamikaze birds. The black cat, only this one is yellow. The flies.

The doorbell rings again and a deep, resonant baritone booms from the murky past, "Mr. John!"

It's Alfonso, the man who used to live next door. The timbre of his voice is identical, but his speech is slurred by false teeth. His sparse hair is disheveled and his skin has an unhealthy sheen. I detect the scent of aguardiente in the air. Alfonso is my age and he used to be my height, though now he looks diminished.

Back then, he'd hang around all day making etchings, strumming the guitar, and trying to stay sober. His wife, a school counselor with a cheerful disposition, had plucked him off the street and gotten him cleaned up. He became her associate in their spiritual advisor business. Sometimes, I'd hear him singing or praying in low tones, and then he'd cry, "Out, Satan!" and accompany the client to her car. With me, he never once broached that subject. Either he knew I was put off by it or he didn't much believe in it himself.

When they had to sell their apartment due to financial straits, Alfonso offered to sell it to us. "I want you and Marta to have it. You can expand your home." At the time it seemed a blessing, but it turned out to be a curse.

"Haven't seen you in years," I tell him.

"I'm in Tumaco now, just visiting. Take a look at this." From a moldy portfolio he produces some etchings. Desertscapes with adobe buildings, cactuses, sand.

"It's not chalk," he sputters. "I use earth, clay."

"Nice," I say, noting a suspicious resemblance to the ones he peddled before, "but who wants to hang nice artwork in a ruin like this?"

"You could just hold on to them."

"I'm not trying to hold on. I'm trying to let go."

"You like this one?" He glances again at the house.

"All right, come on in."

His eyes light up as he enters his former sanctuary, where he was blessed with a roof overhead, food in the fridge, and a kindly woman to tend to his needs. But the light fades as he regards the unfinished concrete floors and luridly exposed pipes, the building materials stacked up along the wall. I sense his disappointment; I've let him down.

"Marta fired the contractor and it's been like this ever since."

"Where's Marta?"

"She died."

"Oh, sorry." He smiles sheepishly. "Listen . . . I need twenty thousand pesos . . ."

As he claps away in his worn-out sandals, furtively counting the bills, I'm struck by the uncanniness of his visit.

Lately I'm haunted by a poem I learned in school. About an ancient, crumbling statue erected in homage to a pharaoh. It goes like this:

"And on the pedestal these words appear: 'My name is Ozymandias, king of kings. Look on my works, ye Mighty, and despair!'

. . . And round the decay of that colossal wreck . . . the lone and level sands stretch far away."

My grandfather, a prosperous businessman who lived to ninety-five, had absolutely nothing to say to me. He was pleasant enough and his handshake could buckle your knees, but he made no attempt to let me in on who he was. To me, he was a mystery and he died a mystery. I vowed I wouldn't turn out like that. But have I kept my vow? Am I the inconsequential old-timer I dreaded I'd become?

Another ghostly voice calls out from the past: Wilson!

When I first saw Marta, she was walking across the campus and I thought she was someone I knew. Strangely, she thought she knew me, as well. We exchanged numbers.

When I knocked at the boarding house where she was living, a voice shouted, "Wil-son!"

A guy in a bathrobe opened the door.

"Is Marta here?" I asked.

"She's coming," he said, and I noted a petulance to his tone. Was he jealous that I had been chosen over him?

One of Marta's regrettable habits was taking a shower without having a towel at hand. For years, when she'd yell at me to bring her one, I'd respond by yodeling, Wilson! Just to keep the joke going, though Marta didn't laugh. It's said that all marriages end up in a power struggle or a relationship of siblings. I would add housemates.

Wilson! I misread you, man. You weren't in love with Marta. Forgetting her towel seemed cute at first, but boy, did it get old. Wilson! Where are you? Why didn't you clue me in?

With the books packed up, all that's left is my work. Articles in journals so piddling they're probably all defunct, and these are likely the last copies that survive. I reach for my first publication, which I authored at twenty-one, and its wilted, stapled pages come to pieces in my hands. Out falls a faded letter notched by typewriter keys. "Congratulations!" it says, "I've been rejecting your professors for years! Enclosed you'll find an honorarium . . ."

I remember driving straight to the bank and waving it at the teller. "I just sold my first article! Want to go out with me to celebrate?" To my astonishment, she said yes, and that night she presented me with a six pack of beer. Miller was the brand, which happened to be her name. Turned out, she had a boyfriend, so things didn't go too far, but that heartfelt gift from Miss Miller seemed to augur a stellar career.

I pack the journals in the box I submitted to Credentials. "Oh, yes," the secretary liked to recall, "you're the one who brought the magazines in the Jack Daniels box."

Venturing out into the hallucinatory heat, I ask the watchman to call for a mover. He has a buddy, even smaller than he, who putters around in a three-wheeled cart.

That's when I see them coming up the street, slow walking in the manner of a solemn procession. The women in flower print dresses, the men in white suits and broad hats. Straight-backed, emanating devotion, they clasp their pious pamphlets as if bearing gifts to an altar.

I quickly turn and go inside.

When things went south with Marta, I found refuge in random affairs. Because I helped the women with their expenses, I worried they were with me just for that. And I worried that they worried I was with them for the other. These attachments all proved finite and, in a way, interchangeable. I loved and mourned them all.

On an impulse, I search for my name on the web. It's an urge I've resisted and I regret giving in. To my alarm, I find no links to my labors, no pictures, no citations, not a trace.

Like words on a blackboard, a life is easily erased.

The driver loads the boxes and I join him in the cab. As I examine his leathery features, I can make out the face he wore when he was young. This is a feat I've perfected with the years, one that a youngster is unable to perform.

The route we travel is one I know like a river knows its course. Yet passing the drug store, the clinic, and the antiquated morgue, encircled rapaciously by undertakers and florists, I feel that I'm seeing them as I did the first time.

The reaction of the students at the entrance to Humanities, many with tattoos that bespeak a new age, seems, paradoxically, both oblivious and suspicious. And it calls to mind a teenage prank, the time when, with friends, we crashed a party of strangers. The surreal sensation of pretending we belonged. The illusion of invisibility, of seeing while unseen, until someone finally asked us who we were. We answered that we had been invited by "Mike." "Mike who?" "Mike Phillips." As they went to inform the host, we slinked out, stifling laughter, and disappeared.

"Wait," says a guard who's face I can't recall. "What's this?"

I present myself as Professor Emeritus.

Perplexed, he confers with the secretaries, whose identities are likewise unclear.

"You can ask the director," I tell him. "She'll know who I am."

"It's a he," says the guard.

A young man who looks like he just started shaving steps forward with a bureaucratic air.

"Oh, yes," he says vaguely at the mention of my name.

"I have a contribution for the book fair."

"Book fair?"

"I received an email . . ."

"Um, I'm afraid . . ."

It suddenly occurs to me that I may have misread the message.

"At any rate, I'm sure they'll be of good use. And my publications can go in the Resource Center."

The director regards the bulging box. Clearly, he's flustered by such a generous gift.

He shifts his weight. "Oh, you don't need to . . ."

"No problem," I say. "No need for thanks."

"Actually, professor" — he moistens his lips — "we're in the process of transitioning to digital. Why don't you wait and I'll take it up with the council."

He excuses himself and I head for the door. I can hear, from the parking lot, the shouts of the guard. "Professor, professor, you left your books in the lobby!"

All my life I believed I was too young to die. I didn't deserve it. It wasn't fair. But now I'm convinced it's the fairest thing of all. The only thing incumbent on every living creature. The final obligation it's our duty to fulfill.

I empty the last closet and the contents of the drawers: a ceramic skull from Acapulco, a keychain with rusty keys. Keys to what? I have no idea.

They're out there again, slow walking toward my door. Armed with their scriptures and sinister smiles. Go away, I mutter, crouching in the shadows. I don't want your preposterous salvation.

The doorbell rings. It's sundown, the cicadas are in full cry. The piquant scent of purple jacarandas, the swarm of gnats around the light.

"Evening, boss," he says, baring his luminous grin.

"I've been waiting for you," I tell him, pointing to my last possessions. "I'll be grateful if you take them off my hands."

Near midnight, as I write the note, the images swirl in my head. I'm pulling a wheelie on my banana seat bike, performing a perfect back flip, racing to the top of the red clay bank aglitter with flecks of fool's gold. I can smell the leather of my baseball glove, the oil of my fishing reel, the calamine lotion like pink frosting on my skin.

I remember the first time, with Mary Margaret Mays, big and buxom and bursting with joy, rocking and creaking on the planks of a boathouse, moonlight on the waves, my senses so inflamed I felt too alive to be alive.

And the fleabag hotel in New York City, where I journeyed to live as a stranger, and challenge myself to a duel with solitude. A condition I considered exclusive to the young. But time has proved me wrong.

The play is nearing the final curtain. The climactic music swells. I'm beset by the feeling that I've fallen out of time.

Of course, there were good years, I write with my grade school lettering. *That's all that one can ask for. So please carry on as if I were never here.*

I cap my pen and check my watch. Now there's nothing to

do but wait. I remind myself that the readiness is all. Any second, the alarm will sound.

Roy Bentley, a finalist for the Miller Williams poetry prize for *Walking with Eve in the Loved City*, is the author of eight books; including *American Loneliness* from Lost Horse Press, who is bringing out a new & selected in 2021. He is the recipient of a Creative Writing Fellowship in Poetry from the National Endowment for the Arts and fellowships from the Florida Division of Cultural Affairs and the Ohio Arts Council. Poems have appeared in *The Southern Review, Guernica, New Letters, Crazyhorse, Shenandoah, Blackbird, Prairie Schooner,* and *Rattle,* among others. A native Ohioan, he lives in Pataskala, Ohio.

K.L. Browne's fiction has appeared or is forthcoming in *Santa Monica Review, Pembroke Magazine, Ascent,* and *PANK Magazine.* She received an MFA from the Bennington Writing Seminars and lives in Mill Valley, California.

Megan E. Calhoun's fiction has appeared in *The Madison Review, The Louisville Review, Lullwater Review,* and *Sententia.* She is currently a freelance editor and a graduate student in Library and Information Science, and lives with her family in Columbus, Ohio.

Maryann Corbett spent 35 years working for the Minnesota Legislature. She's a past winner of the Richard Wilbur Award and the Willis Barnstone Translation Prize, and she's the author of four books of poetry, most recently *Street View* (2017). Her work is published widely, in journals like *The Dark Horse* (UK), *Ecotone, PN Review* (UK), and *Rattle;* in anthologies like *Measure for Measure: An Anthology of Poetic Meters* and *The Best American Poetry 2018;* and online at *The Poetry Foundation.* A fifth book, *In Code,* is due out in 2020.

CATHERINE ESTHER COWIE is a 2017 Callaloo Writing Workshop graduate. Her work has appeared in *Moko Magazine: Caribbean Arts and Letters, The Penn Review, Forklift Ohio, Glass: A Journal of Poetry*, and is forthcoming in *Southern Humanities Review* and *Portland Review*.

LORI D'ANGELO'S work has appeared or is forthcoming in various literary journals, including *Connotation Press, Drunken Boat, Everyday Genius, Forge, Gargoyle, Gravel, Hamilton Stone Review, Hawaii Pacific Review, Heavy Feather Review, Juked, Literary Mama, The New Verse News, r.kv.r.y., Reed Magazine, Stirring: A Literary Collection, TAB*, and *Word Riot*. She is a fellow at Hambidge Center for Creative Arts and Sciences, a grant recipient from the Elizabeth George Foundation, and an alumna of the Squaw Valley Community of Writers Fiction Workshop. She lives in Virginia with her family.

A. KATHRYN DAVIS holds a BA in Creative Writing from a small liberal arts school in Michigan called Grand Valley State, where she served as editor-in-chief of the university's literary journal, *fishladder*. Kathryn currently writes from the southwest corner of Michigan, where she works as a film producer and almost-finishes lots of stories. She can be found on Twitter @kathrvndavis.

ORMAN DAY'S prose and poetry have been published by such journals as *Potomac Review, Creative Nonfiction, ZYZZYVA, Stonecoast, Los Angeles Review, Portland Review*, and *Third Coast*. Following his philosophy that you should accumulate wonderful memories in your youth and recall them with pleasure in your old idle age, he happily recalls dancing the samba in the rain at Carnival, jumping up and down when he won a boat dressed as a frog on *Let's Make a Deal*, and — trying to forget the horrible sunburn that browned his back for six months — skin-diving in the Great Barrier Reef before the coral was bleached by climate change.

JANICE DEAL is currently working on a collection of linked short stories, *Sick Beasts*, which explores the fictional town of Ephrem, Illinois. Her work has won the Cagibi Macaron Prize for Fiction, and has appeared or is forthcoming in magazines including *Fiction*, *The Sun*, *Catamaran Literary Reader*, and *Zone 3*. Her first story collection, *The Decline of Pigeons*, was published by Queen's Ferry Press in 2013. Learn more about her at janicedeal.com.

KATHERINE FALLON'S poems have appeared or are forthcoming in *AGNI*, *Colorado Review*, *Juked*, *Meridian*, *Foundry*, and *Best New Poets 2019*, among others. Her chapbook, *The Toothmakers' Daughters*, is available through Finishing Line Press. She shares domestic space with two cats and her favorite human, who helps her zip her dresses.

RACHAEL GAY is a poet and artist living in Fargo, North Dakota. Her poetry has appeared in journals such as *Anti-Heroin Chic*, *Quail Bell*, *Rag Queens*, *Déraciné Magazine*, *Gramma Poetry*, *FreezeRay Poetry*, *Rising Phoenix Review*, and others, as well as the anthology *What Keeps Us Here* (2019).

PETER GRANDBOIS is the author of ten books, the most recent of which is *half-burnt* (Spuyten Duyvil, 2019). His poems, stories, and essays have appeared in over one hundred journals. His plays have been performed in St. Louis, Columbus, Los Angeles, and New York. He is the Poetry Editor for *Boulevard* magazine and teaches at Denison University in Ohio. You can find him at www. petergrandbois.com.

CONNIE JORDAN GREEN lives on a farm in East Tennessee, where she writes and gardens. She is the author of two award-winning novels for young people, *The War at Home* and *Emmy*, published originally by Margaret McElderry imprint of MacMillan and Simon & Schuster, respectively, reissued in soft cover by Tellico Books imprint of Iris Press; two poetry chapbooks, *Slow Children Playing*, 2007, and *Regret Comes to Tea*, 2011; and two poetry collections, *Household Inventory*, 2015, winner of the Brick Road Poetry Award, and *Darwin's Breath* (Iris Press). Since 1978 she has written a weekly newspaper column for *The Loudon County News Herald*.

MIA HERMAN is a writer and editor living in Queens, NY. Her work has appeared in or is forthcoming in *Atticus Review*, *Barren Magazine*, *Bellevue Literary Review*, *Ghost City Review*, *Literary Mama*, and *Third Coast*, among others. She holds an MFA in Creative Writing from Hofstra University and currently serves as the Associate Managing Editor for *F(r)iction*. When she's not writing or editing, Mia is most likely a) curating road-trip playlists, b) watching obscene amounts of reality TV, or c) setting her friends up on blind dates. Follow her on Twitter @ MiaMHerman.

TIM KEPPEL'S work has appeared in *Glimmer Train*, *The Literary Review*, *Hayden's Ferry Review*, *Notre Dame Review*, *Chicago Quarterly Review*, and elsewhere. The Spanish language version of his story collection, *Where Are You Going?*, was recently published by Penguin Random House in Colombia. Keppel teaches literature and writing at the Universidad del Valle in Cali, Colombia.

HARI BHAJAN KHALSA'S poems have been published in *Poet Lore, Comstock Review, Roanoke Review, Schuylkill Valley Journal, Gyroscope Review, Cathexis Northwest Press,* and *Transcend,* among others, as well as forthcoming in *Quiddity.* She is the author of a chapbook, *Life in Two Parts* (Main Street Rag, 2010) and a book of poems, *Talk of Snow* (Walrus, 2015). She lives in Los Angeles with her husband, just waiting for the perfect dog to join the family.

LISA LOW'S poetry, reviews, interviews, and academic essays have appeared in or are forthcoming in *The Massachusetts Review, The Boston Review, Cross Currents, The Boston Herald, Phoebe, Potomac Review, Crack the Spine, Delmarva Review, Aphros, Broken Plate, Tusculum,* and *Evening Street,* among others. She is one of the editors of *Milton, the Metaphysicals, and Romanticism* (Cambridge University Press, 1994). She received her doctorate in English Literature from University of Massachusetts and spent twenty years as an English professor, teaching at Cornell College; Colby College; and Pace University. In addition to her work as an educator, Low has been a film and theatre critic for *Christian Science Monitor.*

RAYMOND LUCZAK is the author and editor of 22 books, including *Flannelwood* (Red Hen Press) and *Lovejets: Queer Male Poets on 200 Years of Walt Whitman* (Squares & Rebels). He lives in Minneapolis, Minnesota.

AL NYHART received an MFA from the University of Montana and has been a painting contractor for over 40 years. Previous poems have appeared in *Puerto del Sol, Great River Review, Painted Bride Quarterly, North Dakota Review, Wisconsin Review, Berkeley Poetry Review, Whiskey Island, Laurel Review,* and elsewhere. He lives with his wife Cheryl in White Sulphur Springs, Montana.

Alejandro Pérez is a student at Columbia University in New York. He is a 2019 Pushcart Prize nominee whose poems have appeared in *Boulevard*, *The Missouri Review*, *Pacifica Literary Review*, *DIAGRAM*, *Blue Earth Review*, *Salamander*, and Spanish-language magazines in Venezuela, Chile, and Spain. He is currently a staff reader for the poetry teams at both *The Adroit Journal* and *Ploughshares*.

Michael Phillips has published poems and short stories in a variety of journals, including *Philadelphia Stories*, *Tar River Review*, and *Sow's Ear Poetry Review*. He has an MA in English and works for a healthcare research institute. Michael lives in Pennsylvania with his wife, daughter, and new puppy.

Rita Quillen's new novel *Wayland*, a sequel to *Hiding Ezra*, was published by Iris Press in fall, 2019, and her new poetry collection *Some Notes You Hold* is due out from Madville Press in 2020. Her full-length poetry collection, *The Mad Farmer's Wife*, was published in 2016 by *Texas Review* Press, a Texas A&M affiliation, and was a finalist for the Weatherford Award in Appalachian Literature from Berea College. Her novel *Hiding Ezra*, released by Little Creek Books, was a finalist for the 2005 DANA Awards. One of six semi- finalists for the 2012-14 Poet Laureate of Virginia, she received three Pushcart nominations, and a Best of the Net nomination in 2012. Read more at www. ritasimsquillen.com.

Barbara Schwartz is the author of the chapbook *Any Thriving Root* (dancing girl press, 2017) and the hybrid play, *What Survives Is the Fire*, which will be produced by Boomerang Theater in 2020. Her work has appeared in *Nimrod*, *Carolina Quarterly*, *Quiddity*, and elsewhere. She is an educational consultant and lives in Brooklyn.

MICHELE SHARPE, a poet and essayist, is also a high school dropout, hepatitis C survivor, adoptee, and former trial attorney. Her essays are published or forthcoming in *The New York Times, The Rumpus, Guernica, Catapult,* and *The Sycamore Review.* Recent poems can be found in *B O D Y, Rogue Agent, Poet Lore, North American Review, Stirring,* and *Baltimore Review.*

TUFIK SHAYEB'S poetry has appeared in numerous publications, including *Sheepshead Review, The Menteur, Lost Lake Folk Opera, Madcap Review, Heyday Magazine, Blinders Journal, Muzzle Magazine, Restless Anthology, The November 3rd Club,* and others. To date, Shayeb has published three chapbooks and one full-length collection, titled *I'll Love You to Smithereens.* In past years, Shayeb competed in slam poetry competitions and on slam poetry teams, but is currently focused on written word poetry.

TYLER SONES received an MFA from Ohio State in 2019. His work has appeared, or is forthcoming, in *Washington Square Review, Beloit Fiction Journal, Pacifica, SmokeLong Quarterly, Pithead Chapel,* and elsewhere. He lives in Austin, Texas.

JOHN TALBIRD is the author of the chapbook, *A Modicum of Mankind* (Norte Maar). His novel *The World Out There* will be released in 2020 by Madville Publishing, and his fiction and essays have appeared or are forthcoming in *Apalachee Review, Ploughshares, Grain, Juked,* and *North Dakota Quarterly,* among many others. He is a frequent contributor to *Film International,* on the editorial board of *Green Hills Literary Lantern,* and Associate Editor, Fiction, for the noir online journal *Retreats from Oblivion.* A professor at Queensborough Community College — CUNY, he lives with his wife in New York City.

ANNE HUNLEY TRISLER'S poetry has appeared in *Connotation Press, The Sow's Ear Poetry Review, Wild Goose Poetry Review, Glass Mountain, Dash Literary Journal, Black Fox Literary Magazine,* and elsewhere. This year her work was featured in Z Publishing House's 2019 Best Emerging Poets series. She lives in Knoxville, Tennessee, where she is pursuing an MFA in Poetry at the University of Tennessee. She can be reached at atrisler@vols.utk.edu.

LOUISE WHITE lives and writes in Annapolis on Maryland's Chesapeake Bay. Her poems have been published in *Life in Me Like Grass on Fire* (Maryland Writers' Association Books), *Bay Weekly, The Northern Virginia Review, UP.ST. ART Annapolis Magazine, The Skinny Poetry Journal,* and *Grub Street Literary Magazine.* With three other Maryland poets, she published a chapbook, *Thursday's Quartet.* She meets weekly with fellow poets in the Women Poets Workshop, which stems from the Maryland Writers' Association. She has just completed a rigorously edited chapbook collection, *Dear Peace Corps, I Thought You'd Want to Know.*

SARAH WYMAN writes and teaches on verbal / visual intersections in the Hudson Valley, where climbing feet kick dust down to a river-sea. Her work has appeared in *Aaduna, Mudfish, Quarry, Petrichor Review, A Slant of Light: Contemporary Women Poets of the Hudson Valley* (Codhill), and other venues. Finishing Line Press published her chapbook *Sighted Stones* last year.

www.ingramcontent.com/pod-product-compliance
Lightning Source LLC
Chambersburg PA
CBHW031957170626
46807CB00006B/2534